NEW ITALIAN POETS

《》

NEW ITALIAN POETS

edited by

DANA GIOIA & MICHAEL PALMA

《》

STORY LINE PRESS
1991

First American Printing

ACKNOWLEDGEMENTS

Some of these translations have appeared in periodicals, including *Poetry, The New Yorker, Wigwag, Chronicles, William and Mary Review, Paris Review, Painted Bride Quarterly, Raddle Moon, Sulfur,* and *Porch.* Grateful acknowledgement is made to those editors.

Library of Congress Catalog Card Number:
90-52855

ISBN: 0-934257-42-6

Book design by Lysa McDowell

Published by Story Press, Inc.
d.b.a. Story Line Press
Three Oaks Farm
Brownsville, OR
97327-9718

For

William Jay Smith and Felix Stefanile

two noble kinsmen

VALERIO MAGRELLI

INTRODUCTION

BY DANA GIOIA

New Italian Poets is not a comprehensive anthology of contemporary Italian verse. There is too much recent Italian poetry of real interest to be contained in a single collection. Rather than trying to map out the entire poetic landscape of current Italian literature, this anthology presents an extensive selection of the work of ten influential writers. The decision to focus the volume on a few poets necessarily excluded many deserving writers. One could easily list a dozen important poets not included in this volume (such as Amelia Rosselli or Giuseppe Conte). But the editors felt more would be gained in depth than lost in range. To cover the broader literary scene would have limited the anthology to two or three brief poems by each author. Presenting so many unfamiliar poets so cursorily would have been extraordinarily confusing to American readers. Poems would have blurred together, and, robbed of individuality, the poets would have become little more than a list of interchangeable foreign names. Instead, by focusing the anthology on a few younger and middle-aged writers, *New Italian Poets* allows the reader the space to get to know each author reasonably well.

Although the poets in this anthology represent the diverse trends of contemporary Italian literature, one important area has been excluded—dialect poetry. Even today nearly every Italian speaks a local dialect in addition to standard *Toscano*. This everyday, familial, spoken language helps define and preserve the communal identity of each region, and interesting

INTRODUCTION

poetry (as well as song) continues to be written in various dialects. Translating dialect poetry into English, especially American English, presents enormous theoretical and practical difficulties. Not only do few Americans master any Italian dialect well enough to understand its nuances, but there are also no satisfactory linguistic equivalents in current American English. Surely the awkward and flavorless versions one occasionally sees of contemporary poems in dialect give new meaning to the old Italian saying, *traduttore/traditore*. Rather than provide unsatisfactory versions of dialect poets, this anthology has left this rich area of Italian literature to the specialists. Once again the editorial principle has been to avoid clutter, however well-intentioned, and focus the collection on what could be done well.

But while explaining what has been excluded, there is no need to apologize for what *New Italian Poets* contains. The anthology introduces American readers to two generations of Italian poets, none of whom has previously been translated into English at any length. The first writer in the collection, Maria Luisa Spaziani (born 1924), is somewhat older than the others, but she is a poet of international importance who is virtually unknown in the U.S. Since she was one of the first women to win a major place in the still male-dominated world of Italian poetry, her reputation developed more slowly than those of her contemporaries, and so she is not entirely out of place in this gathering of younger writers. More important, her work,

INTRODUCTION

with its hard-edged lyricality, musical resonance, emotional directness, and apolitical thematics, in many ways signalled the change of sensibility reflected by the younger poets in this volume.

Spaziani is followed by Rossana Ombres, Rodolfo Di Biasio, Fabio Doplicher, Umberto Piersanti, and Luigi Fontanella, who were born before or during the Second World War. They represent the dominant middle-generation of contemporary Italian poets. The collection ends with the work of four exceptionally talented younger poets—Patrizia Cavalli, Paolo Ruffilli, Milo De Angelis, and Valerio Magrelli—all born after the war. Their extraordinarily diverse work demonstrates the variety of new poetry now being written in Italy.

Italian critics characteristically discuss contemporary poetry in terms of schools and movements. Reading the histories of twentieth-century Italian poetry, an American sometimes feels that the world of high art has been described in the manner of high fashion. Poetry becomes a dazzling parade of ephemeral literary trends—Twilight Poetry, Futurism, Hermeticism, Realistic Experimentalism, Fourth Generation, the Lombardian Line, Group '63. Even today the Italian critical mind remains classical and Aristotelian. All new poets must be neatly grouped, named, and classified. In post-war Italy there has also been a compulsive critical tendency to link emerging poetic movements with the past. Like parents who dress their younger children in hand-me-down clothes, Italian critics frugally refurbish old

3

theories to describe new poets. No other modern literature displays so many "neo" movements—New Realism, New Lyricism, New Experimentalism, New Avant-Garde, New Hermeticism, New Twilight Poetry, and the ultimate in novelty—*i Novissimi*. One sometimes feels that Italy has more poetic schools than soccer teams.

While poetic schools have proven useful for emerging writers in gaining public attention and inspiring critical commentary, they often have limited utility in helping a reader understand the poems themselves. Critical generalizations about a new poetic trend, however accurate, usually have more relevance to a particular movement's average poems than to its most enduring ones. What makes a superb poem work is often its ability to defy easy categorization. Likewise, talented poets too frequently change direction to be adequately defined by a fixed formula. A theory that might have helped clarify one moment in their development no longer applies to their later work. Nor is it difficult for a student of Italian literature to find a poem by a member of one school which perfectly satisfies the rules of another movement.

For reasons of cultural politics Italian critics often define literary groups according to extra-literary criteria. Poets may be assigned to a particular school more on the basis of a personal friendship or common publication than because of a shared aesthetic. Sandro Penna, for instance, is sometimes considered a hermetic poet, although his style displays an exemplary clar-

INTRODUCTION

ity and his subject matter foreshadows that of neo-realism. Likewise Dino Campana, whose visionary poetry reached for symbolic rather than political transformations, has been linked for biographical rather than aesthetic reasons with the *Vociani* group, which was committed to social reform and moral enlightenment.

Following critical practice, most anthologies of Italian poetry group their authors into literary schools. *New Italian Poets*, however, resists the custom. This anthology presents its authors as individuals. While poets sometimes emerge in schools, the best ones rarely remain true to a common aesthetic. Likewise, contemporary critical labels are too simplistic to explain the best work now being written. How reductive, for instance, to classify Spaziani as a feminist poet. Surely the hard-won lessons of feminism stand behind the framework of her poetry, but Spaziani's vision is essentially aesthetic, not social. And her voice—despite its unmistakably contemporary accent—can be heard conversing in tones of affectionate equality with the overwhelmingly male tradition of Italian lyric poetry. It is similarly misleading to term Magrelli a "neo-crepuscular" poet because his work focuses on commonplace events. The more striking feature of Magrelli's work is its sheer originality. The purpose of *New Italian Poets* is not to create literary genealogies or map out competing camps. The anthology merely seeks to present worthy poets well translated in a format which lets American readers concentrate directly on the poems themselves

INTRODUCTION

without too many critical preconceptions.

Even in an anthology as focused as *New Italian Poets*, however, there may be some initial difficulties for an American reader. Poetry in Italian and English has been so closely interrelated over the past four centuries that an American sometimes forgets the degree to which Italian poetry continues to be a foreign literary tradition. While not ignoring the similarities between the literatures, an American reader approaching this anthology needs to keep in mind some of the critical differences between the situation and direction of poetry in the two cultures.

Although to some degree every modern literature possesses an international element, poetry remains essentially national in its character. A country's poetry may borrow elements from other literatures, but it usually adapts them in a distinctive and original way. Always a sophisticated, even learned art, poetry is nonetheless primitive in its tribal impulse. Rooted in the language, history, and customs of a particular people, each poetic tradition moves according to its own internal rhythms. Although traditions frequently intersect, they never run parallel for long.

Modernism, for instance, was a relatively brief episode in British poetry. Provoked mainly by London-based Irishmen and Americans, it flourished from 1914 through the late 1930's (during which time it paradoxically coexisted with the traditional Georgian poetry). But in Italian poetry modernism began explo-

INTRODUCTION

sively in 1909 with F.T. Marinetti's Futurist Manifesto and only seventy years later did it begin to lose vigor. Likewise Romanticism, which still casts a powerful spell over English-language poetry, scarcely exists for an Italian reader to whom the 19th century is the age of *Il Risorgimento*. The Italian Romantic genius expressed itself primarily in opera, not in poetry, which remained rooted in classicism.

Even the way a reader in one nation views a writer of another country often differs from how a native might see that author. For romance-language readers the most influential poet of English Romanticism is not Coleridge, Wordsworth, Blake or Keats, but Byron. Likewise a Frenchman or Italian would consider Goethe Germany's greatest Romantic poet. But to a German, Goethe has little to do with Romanticism. Writers are viewed differently from within the context of their own culture than they are from beyond. The scholar's task is to recreate that cultural and temporal context. The importance of such scholarly effort is self-evident when discussing the literature of the past, but in subtler ways it is necessary even when approaching foreign poetry of our own era, which often requires cultural as well as linguistic translation.

Although neither Italian or American poets currently command a large readership, they do have somewhat different assumptions about their audience. Over the past half century in America there has grown up a national network of institutions to support poetry—creative writing programs, writers' conferences, artists' colonies, reading series, as well as a myriad of literary magazines and small presses. Based mostly in the university, this literary network does not reach the general public, but it has fostered a thriving underground culture for contemporary poetry. Most American poets now work somewhere in this subculture, usually teaching creative writing, and established writers enjoy a sizable professional audience of fellow poets and their students. Poetry books and journals are published in unprecedented numbers, but the most important means of reaching this specialized audience is the poetry reading, a cultural ritual that has had an immense impact on current American poetry.

Italian poets have a different relationship to their audience. Creative writing programs do not exist in Italy. Consequently there is no established institutional audience of students and instructors. Most poets do not teach, and those who do work mostly in standard academic subjects like philosophy or classics. Well-known poets give public readings, but since there is no extensive network of academic support, such appearances occur infrequently, usually at festivals and conferences. Compared to that of America, Italian intellectual life is less closely identified with the university. Most poets still live in a bohemia of artists and intellectuals.

Part of a non-specialized intellectual community, the Italian poet remains actively involved in both ideas and ideologies. If the American archetypes of the poet are the vagabond bard

INTRODUCTION

(like Whitman or Lindsay) and the tragic misfit (like Poe or Dickinson), the Italian image is the scholarly but socially committed man of letters. Since Dante and Petrarch, Italian poets have been conspicuously learned individuals. They have also been politically active even when that involvement put them in exile, like Dante, or in prison, like Pavese. Poets have not insisted on being separate from society. Instead they belong to both the conscience and consciousness of their culture. Italy has also traditionally honored its artists and intellectuals. Even today well-known writers enjoy great social status. Consequently Italian poets have always been comfortable with their identity as members of an artistic intelligentsia.

American literature, reflecting the values of its society, has always had an anti-intellectual streak. From Twain to Hemingway, from Whitman to Williams, the artist has often tried to identify more closely with the common man than the learned one. Too much education is frequently seen as a sign of remoteness from life. An American reader therefore needs to understand how natural intellectuality is to an Italian artist. Poetry is still a legitimate means of philosophical inquiry, and epistemology is an essential enterprise of modern verse. Yet the resulting poetry is not abstract or academic. Valerio Magrelli's philosophical speculations, for example, unfold with sensual specificity—just as his erotic explorations turn naturally into figures of thought. Likewise Milo De Angelis' concentrated and hermetic poems achieve a remarkable lyric momentum and

INTRODUCTION

emotional power.

Intellectual life always includes politics, and in this century Italy's political upheavals have posed inescapable problems to its poets. Cultural debates have inevitably involved political issues (such as the fierce critical battles between the hermetic and neo-realist poets). Although some poets tried to keep their literary and political identities separate, this distinction was difficult to maintain in a nation where most poets worked as journalists. Most post-war Italian poetry was saturated with politics, and writers like Pier Paolo Pasolini and Cesare Pavese became public figures. Yet this cultural situation has unexpectedly changed over the last two decades. Perhaps the intensity of Italy's postwar ideological maelstrom eventually exhausted younger artists. Or the growing prosperity of contemporary Italy blunted the social urgency of earlier political agenda. For whatever reasons, the new generation of poets appears less overtly political than their immediate predecessors. Instead of the ferocious partisan politics of the 1950's and 1960's, one sees subtler and more personal critiques of society. The narratives of Rossana Ombres may imply a radical revision of sexual and familial identities, or the apocalyptic imagery of Fabio Doplicher protest the alienation inherent in post-industrial society, but the author's politics usually remain in the subtext rather than determining the poem's overt thematics. This new generation seems to signal a political transformation in Italian cultural life. Poetry has finally escaped the burdens of modern

INTRODUCTION

history. The organized struggles of earlier writers have earned the contemporary poet the luxury of privacy and independence.

But Italian political and cultural history has brought the poet to a different place from the literary landscape an American writer now takes for granted. Still rooted in modernism, the Italian writer assumes the poem's right to be challenging and difficult. Forty years of public poetry readings have worked to simplify most contemporary American poetry. It is now generally more personal and accessible than the verse of the modernist generation. But Italians still write mainly for the page. Not only international modernism but also the native tradition of hermeticism still influences contemporary practice. The short, self-referential poem—a text that demands to be seen as well as heard—remains as much in the mainstream today (as in the work of Milo De Angelis or Valerio Magrelli) as it was sixty years ago with Giuseppe Ungaretti or Salvatore Quasimodo. The tone and manner of such verse may differ from earlier models. Magrelli is often wryly humorous, and Patrizia Cavalli fiercely emotional. But the impulse to concentrate and intensify poetry to the utmost degree endures. One sees this tendency to work in luminous miniatures even in an expansive writer like Paolo Ruffilli, who builds his long poems out of mysterious but memorable fragments.

Even if an Italian poet's political orientation is no longer at issue, his intellectual obligations abide. Italian poetry remains more concerned with philosophical and cultural issues than American verse. Consequently it is less determinedly personal and autobiographical. The poetry of both traditions celebrates the individual, but for Americans it is the naive and unspoiled side of the poet that usually takes precedence, whereas for Italians it is the wise and worldly aspect. Italy is a country too old and battle-scarred to afford unqualified innocence.

If American literature still prizes sincerity and authenticity, Italian values realism and intellectual honesty. To compare the classics of the tradition that created *The Adventures of Tom Sawyer* and *Leaves of Grass* with the one exemplified by *The Divine Comedy* and *The Decameron* is to understand how differently the underlying currents of each culture flow, no matter how often their waters mix. (Or in popular culture contrast two minor masterpieces—Walt Disney's luminously sweet *Pinocchio* and Carlo Collodi's hard-boiled original.) One tradition produces—to choose two poets of radically divergent styles— Edna St. Vincent Millay and William Carlos Williams. The same era in Italy fosters Eugenio Montale and Salvatore Quasimodo. Even in today's Americanized Italy, the poet remains a public intellectual doomed or blessed with the task of elucidating the individual's place in an ancient but still changing culture. Catholicism has largely disappeared as a direct influence on Italian poetry (except as cultural detritus to be exploited savagely as in Ruffilli's work), but the spiritual discipline of its religious training endures. Catholic spirituality has often been obsessed with the body, and Italian poetry, therefore, takes for granted that all ideas, however abstract, must ultimately be reconciled with the flesh.

Just as political ideologies have relaxed in Italian poetry, so too have literary ones. As in America, a diversity of styles is now open to Italian poets. One sees rhyme and meter cautiously returning after nearly half a century of absence. Maria Luisa Spaziani often works in rhyme. Luigi Fontanella, who has made a virtue of eclecticism, also uses it on occasion. (In discussing the differences between current Italian and American poetic practice, a critic might look on Luigi Fontanella, who has spent much of his adult life in literary America, as an exemplary anomaly. While teaching in the U.S., Fontanella has developed a trans-Atlantic poetic idiom which—in its autobiographical concerns, conversational tone, and eschewal of modernist elements—more closely resembles American models than Italian ones.) Meanwhile Umberto Piersanti has revived the traditional hendecasyllabic line for his long lyric odes, but he employs it controversially in a loose and fluid manner. Paolo Ruffilli's mosaic methodology, which unites fragments of wildly different styles, frequently uses rhyme to stunning effect. Ruffilli's experimental work voraciously includes traditional elements in a way the neo-avant-garde verse of the 1960's did not. The popularity of Ruffilli's difficult poems shows the changes in contemporary taste where an eclectic empiricism has replaced literary ideology as the guiding principle. Italian poets no longer have to renounce every element of the past to claim their place in the present.

The achievements of twentieth-century Italian poetry have been extraordinarily rich. No other European country can surpass—and few can equal—the virtuosity and depth of modern Italian verse. Nor has any era in Italian literature since the Renaissance produced so many major poets in so short a span—D'Annunzio, Marinetti, Gozzano, Saba, Campana, Ungaretti, Montale, Quasimodo, Pavese, Luzi, Pasolini, Zanzotto—as well as many distinguished minor ones. The vitality of this modernist tradition continues, even as it moves beyond modernism. New Italian poetry seeks to reconcile experiment with accessibility, intellectuality with passion, an elitist past with a populist future. Where this synthesis will end no one knows, but surely the writers of the new generation have made an exciting beginning.

MARIA LUISA SPAZIANI

'MARIA LUISA SPAZIANI

CRITICAL NOTE

Maria Luisa Spaziani was born in 1924 in Turin and was educated there, writing a dissertation on Marcel Proust. She moved to Rome in 1957 and has lived there ever since. She describes herself as "also part Sicilian," because for the past twenty-five years she has taught French language and literature at the University of Messina. Her literary career, now spanning forty years, has been both varied and distinguished. Virtually all of her many books of poetry have won awards. The most recent, *La stella del libero arbitrio* (The Free-Willed Star, 1986), received three prizes. Her poetry has been translated into eighteen languages, and a collected edition was published by Mondadori in 1979. She has also written criticism, fiction, drama, radio and television scripts, and a musical libretto. In 1973, she edited the French edition of Dino Campana's *Canti orfici (Orphic Songs,* 1914), a central text of the modernist movement in early twentieth-century Italian poetry. Spaziani has also published sixteen volumes of translations from English, German, and especially French. She has translated three books each by Marguerite Yourcenar and Michel Tournier, as well as work by Goethe, George Sand, André Gide, and Jean Cocteau, among many others. Her versions of three tragedies by the seventeenth-century playwright Jean Racine have, like Richard Wilbur's English translations of the same author, retained the rhyming couplets of the originals.

MARIA LUISA SPAZIANI

The poetry of Maria Luisa Spaziani displays an extraordinary unity of tone, style, and sensibility. Her successive volumes show no sudden turns or leaps, but rather a constant, quiet refinement and enrichment of her art. While some poets flaunt a conscious sense of their own newness and break, often defiantly, with their predecessors, Spaziani smoothly incorporates her poetic heritage and carefully builds upon it (critics have professed to find in her work the influences of poets as disparate as Rilke, Eugenio Montale, and Dylan Thomas). While her poems are fluent and accessible on the surface, their achievement is subtle and often paradoxical. With their solid craft and shapely appearance, their recurring (and often surprising) patterns of rhyme, and (in her later work) their long-lined quatrains, the poems seem to seek through art itself to compensate for the evanescence and insubstantiality that they so often describe. Despite the rich and colorful imagery, despite the precise landscapes in which dreams and memories are rooted, in the end all is "pure dust." And yet the final irony is perhaps a hopeful one. That insubstantiality, so often the cause of desolation in other poets, may be here a saving grace. What transcends the physical outlives it, and as the poet says, "passion is too important a ghost to be made flesh."

—M.P.

18

MARIA LUISA SPAZIANI

POETRY

Le acque del sabato. Milan, 1954.

Primavera a Parigi. Milan, 1954.

Luna Lombarda. Vicenzo, 1959.

Il gong. Milan, 1962.

Utilità della memoria. Milan, 1966.

L'occhio del ciclone. Milan, 1970.

Ultrasuoni. Lugano, 1976.

Transito con catene. Milan, 1977.

Poesie. Milan, 1979.

Geometria del disordine. Milan, 1981.

La stella del libero arbitrio. Milan, 1986.

Giovanna d'Arco. Milan, 1990.

CONVENTO NEL '45

Tempo di viole bianche: e sui declivi
la neve agonizzava,
gli abeti trafiggevano il turchino,
sopra i poveri deschi
i frati salmodiavano in latino
e la valle in trionfo si striava
di fughe di tedeschi.

Tempo di viole bianche, ardua scalata
di giovinezza ai varchi dell'istante.
Mi abbagli ancora, scaglia di diamante,
impero incontrastato della rosa
in cima all'erta di trifogli freschi

(né alcuno mai ci disse che la dolce
Collina dell'Amata
tanto cresciuta nell'ultimo anno
era soltanto—o giovanile inganno—
un cumulo di teschi).

(1966)

MARIA LUISA SPAZIANI

THE CONVENT IN '45

Time of white violets; and on the slopes
the snow was dying,
the spruces were piercing turquoise skies,
over their humble suppers
the friars were singing in Latin,
and the valley was furrowed triumphantly
with the flight of the Germans.

Time of white violets, youth's
arduous climb to the threshold of the moment.
You stun me still, you diamond flake,
uncontested realm of the rose
at the summit of the fresh clover slope

(nor did anyone ever tell us that the sweet
Hill of the Beloved,
grown so large the year before,
was only—oh youthful illusion—
a heap of skulls).

(Beverly Allen)

PURA POLVERE

Di qui è passato il Tasso? Sant'Onofrio
grigio nel vento, a marzo, da un muretto
mi porse a consolarmi una mimosa
gracile, dove i bocci d'avvenire
erano grani di sabbia minuta.
Il Tevere spingeva onde di fango,
ma fango senza linfa, pura polvere,
e io col fiato mozzo, con quel fiato
orrendo dell'angoscia che non giunge
a ossigenare il fondo dei polmoni,
guardavo, a me terribilmente simile,
un vecchio che portava in un giornale
mucchi di cicche spente.

Di qui è passato...? Come mortalmente
certuni vanno per le strade, e il canto
della speranza è rombo misterioso,
codice senza chiave. Preme in alto
la cupola di bronzo, siamo spenti
solitari animali che si fissano
(per non morire) mete umili, certe,
la circolare rossa, poi la cena.
L'attesa di una lettera dà in gola

PURE DUST

Is this where Tasso walked? Old Sant'Onofrio
grey with the wind, in March, from out a wall
puts forth a new mimosa to console me,
graceful where the buds to come
were grains of minute sand.
The Tiber pushed its waves of mud,
but lymphless mud, pure dust,
and I, with bated breath,
that horrid anguished breath that does not sweep
its air into the bottom of our lungs,
was watching someone terribly like me,
an old man who was carrying in a paper
countless butts of cigarettes.

Is this where...? As some people
walk fatally through the streets, the song
of hope an eerie rumble all the while,
a code without a key. Pressing down from up on high,
the cupola of bronze, and we are spent,
solitary creatures, setting goals
both humble and secure (so as not to die):
the tramway home, then supper.
To wait for a letter brings a lump

piccoli strappi duri, da catena,
e il Tevere rivolge la sua polvere
senza guizzi o scintille, senza inviti
a fondare città...

(1966)

MARIA LUISA SPAZIANI

—a chain-like hard constriction—to our throat,
and the Tiber churns and churns its dust
with no leaps or flashes, with no invitations
to found new cities...

(Beverly Allen)

MARIA LUISA SPAZIANI

Se fosse un mare questo vento immenso
che sconvolge gli abeti, che scoperchia
le tombe al cimitero, che scompiglia
nuvole e formicai, se fosse un mare,
quest'arca in cui viviamo affronterebbe
il delirio e il naufragio. Eppure il peso
della pietra, quest'ancora che affonda
nel centro stesso della terra, è forte
molto più del groviglio di radici
che da cent'anni frenano la quercia.
Certo molto va a fondo, molte scaglie
e cellule defunte si trasporta
lontano, a sera, il vento tempestoso.
Ma non più d'altri giorni, e se la nera
mano che scerpa i tetti qui mi lascia
di te l'intatto volto, è segno certo
che anche la quercia accanto a te è un fuscello.
Forse mi salva la grazia del tuo nome.
Ma forse tutto è favola, e ammantato
da una calma suprema,
non sei altro che l'occhio del ciclone.

(1970)

MARIA LUISA SPAZIANI

If it were a sea, this immense wind
that shoots through the spruces, splays open
the cemetery tombs, scrambles
the clouds and the ant-hills, if it were a sea,
this ark we live in would face
delirium and shipwreck. And yet the weight
of the stone, this anchor sinking
to the earth's very core, is much
stronger than the tangle of roots
stifling the oak for a hundred years now.
It drives deep, deep, yes. Traveling far of an evening,
the storm wind sucks away
dead scales, dead cells.
But no more than on other days, and if the black
hand that strips off the roofs here leaves me
your face intact, it's a sure sign
that even the oak next to you is just straw.
Maybe your name, its grace, spares me.
But maybe all this is a fable, and you, mantled
in supreme calm,
are, in fact, simply the eye of the cyclone.

(Beverly Allen)

La tua vita e un bambino ancor non nato,
bosco che dorme sotto tanta neve.
Libro bianco nel mondo di Platone
in attesa di chi nasca per scriverlo.
La tua vita è il Tirreno di febbraio
senza tempeste, inerte, dai fondali
pullulanti di uova la cui sorte
si affida al buio genio delle sabbie.
Ma ogni tramonto sfoglia un calendario
invisibile in cielo, e già si annuncia
ai miei occhi che vedono ben oltre
le cortine del giorno, il misterioso
peso astrale che piega la bilancia
ai fasti dell'estate, a san Giovanni,
quando ogni fibra ascolta con tremore
l'arrivo della trave incandescente
e ne sfrigola l'onda delirante
e ne vibra da un polo all'altro il mare
tutto in ardore.

(1979)

MARIA LUISA SPAZIANI

Your life is a baby not yet born,
a forest sleeping under deep snow.
In Plato's world, a blank white book
awaiting the birth of someone who'll write it.
Your life is the Tyrrhenian Sea in February,
stormless, inert, where the depths
teem with spawn whose fate
depends on the dark guardianship of the sands.
But every sunset ruffles through the heavens'
unseen calendar, and already the weight appears
—my eyes see far beyond
the day's curtains—the mysterious
astral weight that tilts the scales
toward summer's celebrations, toward San Giovanni,
when every tendril trembles, listening for
the nearing incandescent plow-beam
that comes to crackle the raving wave
and vibrate the earth's waters
all ablaze.

(Beverly Allen)

Roma ha mille fontane, e a maggio cantano
e scrosciano, pontificano e tuonano
quasi che il mare non lontano irrompa
per le bocche segrete. Dee, titani,
divinità fluviali, tartarughe
e angeli e conchiglie e cornucopie.
Forse la verità, sempre taciuta,
è che ogni strada, piazza o vicoletto,
pur con palazzi, erme ed obelischi
e cattedrali e stadi, sia una crosta
sottilissima, un mare di sargassi
quasi sul punto di smembrarsi e cedere.
Il mare è là, è qui, bolle furioso
da queste spie con voci di sirena.
Chiama all'antica patria, risuona,
fruscia di perle e di meduse,
ci annuncia al regno delle Madri, appresta
per qualche oscuro fato i suoi fondali,
le sue grotte di musica, i suoi archi
di tenebra e trionfo.

(1979)

MARIA LUISA SPAZIANI

Rome has a thousand fountains, and in May they sing
and gurgle, pontificate and thunder
as if the not too distant sea were bursting
through their secret mouths. Goddesses, titans,
river divinities, turtles
and angels and shells and cornucopias.
Maybe the truth, always suppressed,
is that every street, piazza or alleyway,
even the ones with palaces, herms and obelisks
and cathedrals and stadiums, is an incredibly fragile
crust, a sargasso sea
just on the verge of coming undone and giving up.
The sea is there, the sea is here, boiling furiously
out from these siren-voiced peepholes.
It calls to the ancient country, it resounds,
it rustles with pearls and jellyfish,
it announces the reign of the Mothers, by some obscure fate,
it readies its depths,
its music-filled grottoes, its archways
of shadow and triumph.

(Beverly Allen)

MARIA LUISA SPAZIANI

VIA MARGUTTA
a F. F.

Grigi cortili dove la magnolia
imprigionata suda la sua pena.
In alto il Pincio, come una carena,
punta a occidente ma non parte mai.
Tu che cammini in queste strade, sai
la vita brulicante dei fondali.
Forse fu errore cercare le ali,
solo in fondo la perla troverai.
Trentasei anni. Il numero bruciante
brucia te solo, ma il cielo l'ignora.
Benché in catene la magnolia sboccia
e la tua sorte nemmeno la sfiora.
Sarà un corallo forse, e non lo sa,
e saranno conchiglie le sue viole.
Una penombra già sottomarina
ci insegna, tutti, a diffidar del sole.
Trentasei anni. Un occhio di polena,
arso dal sole, vede ciò che vuole.

(1979)

VIA MARGUTTA
to F. F.

Grey courtyards where the imprisoned
magnolia sweats out its sentence.
Above, the Pincio hill, like a ship,
aims toward the west but never departs.
You who walk in these streets, you know
how the depths swarm with life.
Maybe it was a mistake to search for wings,
you'll find the pearl only at the bottom.
Thirty six years. The burning number
burns you alone, but the sky doesn't notice.
Even though it's in chains, the magnolia blooms,
and your fate doesn't even brush against it.
Maybe it's a coral without realizing it,
and maybe its violets are shells.
A shadow, already submerged,
teaches us all to mistrust the sun.
Thirty six years. A figurehead's eye,
burnt by the sun, sees whatever it wants to.

(Beverly Allen)

MARIA LUISA SPAZIANI

Tenero cuore, muscolo peloso,
avrai la forza di gridare al vento
che festa fu quel giorno (ancor non nato)
quando impazzita scese dagli alpini
valichi incontrastati la ruggente
torma degli elefanti che i boschetti
sacri ai tuoi dei con gaia apocalisse
andavano schiacciando? (Quanti secoli
occorrevano a fare del mio cuore
un ben lustro musco?) Ora la turba
degli odoacri s'è accampata all'ombra
dei Fori e a notte sul biancore pario
danzano polverose caracalle
ebbre di ritmi barbari. La luna
sale dall'Aventino e tutto inonda
del suo latte di favola, serena,

né alcun editto ancora l'ha avvertita
che indubbiamente resta un astro, ma
come dea, è finita.

(1979)

MARIA LUISA SPAZIANI

Tender heart, hairy muscle,
are you strong enough to cry to the wind
that happy was the day (not yet born)
when, crazed, down from the Alpine
slopes descended uncontested the bellowing
herd of elephants as they crushed
the woods sacred to your gods
with blithe apocalypse? (How many centuries
did it take to make my heart
such a lustrous museum?) Now the Ottokar hoards
are encamped in the shade
of the Forums and at night on the Parian marble whiteness
they dance up dusty caracallas
drunk with barbarous rhythms. The moon
rises from the Aventine and bathes everything
in her fairy-tale milk, serene,

nor has any edict informed her as yet
that undoubtedly she remains a heavenly body, but,
as a goddess, she's done for.

(Beverly Allen)

MARIA LUISA SPAZIANI

BIANCO SU BIANCO

Il miele notturno che plana dalle ali del Pincio
fruga scompiglia le mie remote nebulose,
agita defunte bandiere, impollina controsperanza
le immagini-idee che hanno per stemma il tuo nome.

E tu, mia disturbata sinfonia, affresco che la lebbra corrode,
béviti quest'orgia silenziosa, affronta la confessione.
Sei stato vivo, sei stato vero, hai respirato un giorno?
Potevano morderti i cani, hai bevuto a sorgenti terrene?

Tutto è bianco su bianco, fantasma, leggenda o follia,
fata morgana, Amleto, delirio di febbre ventenne.
Non fa ombra il tuo corpo più del vento di marzo,
e lasci sul cuore orme più leggere della faina.

(1979)

MARIA LUISA SPAZIANI

WHITE ON WHITE

The nocturnal honey that glides down from the flanks
    of the Pincio hill
ruffles through and messes up my distant nebulosities,
it shakes out defunct flags and pollinates against all hope
the image-ideas that have your name as their coat-of-arms.

As for you, my troubled symphony, my leprosy-corroded
    fresco,
drink in this silent orgy, I tell you, face up to confession.
Were you ever alive, were you ever real, did you ever
    draw a breath?
Could dogs have bitten you, did you ever drink the
    waters of this earth?

Everything is white on white, ghost, legend, or madness,
fata morgana, Hamlet, the delirium of a feverish
    twenty-year-old.
Your body leaves no more shadow than the March wind,
and you leave footprints on my heart lighter than a doe's.

(Beverly Allen)

LA POLENA

Lunga notte di tigli, le tue dita di miele
raspavano ventose fino a staccare le stelle.
La bella arca amorosa volgeva a oscuri mari
fra smemoranti ondate le sue vele.

Io scavavo nel buio quei regni sublunari,
tendevo al mio destino esili ragnatele.
Care ombre placate, relitti di corsari,
non sfiori il vostro fiato queste sere.

Un tempo (già passato?) la sua più azzurra vena
era il leggio segreto di un foglio troppo bianco.
Quest'altra giovinezza ha sguardo di polena,
turba e travolge un timoniere stanco.

(1979)

THE FIGUREHEAD

Long night of linden trees, your honey hands
were scraping like wind trying to unstick the stars.
Love's beautiful ark was turning its sails
among forgetful swells toward dark seas.

I excavated those sublunar kingdoms in the dark,
I offered thin spiderwebs to my fate.
My dear, placated ghosts, you pirates' wrecks,
let not your breath graze these evenings.

Once (already in the past?), his bluest vein
was a secret book-stand for a page that was too white.
This other youthfulness has the gaze of a figurehead
that overturns and sweeps away a weary helmsman.

(Beverly Allen)

LA COMETA

Quel mio amore per lui aveva ali di cera—
lunghe le ali sembravano eterne—
battevano il cielo sicure, sfioravano picchi,
puntavano al sole con nervature nervine—

Fuse le ali ormai mi ricrescono dentro,
soltanto ora perdute mi diventano vere,
e ai cuori incauti grido: *la passione è un fantasma*
troppo importante, uomini, per potersi incarnare —

Chiomate vaganti comete di Halley, presagi
disastri prodigi che infiammano e gelano il sangue,
nessuno osi fissarvi, si arrischi a sfiorare
coaguli di pura lontananza—morgane

(1986)

MARIA LUISA SPAZIANI

THE COMET

That love of mine for him had waxen wings—
they were so long they seemed eternal—
with confidence, they beat the sky, grazed the peaks,
thrust toward the sun with nervine nets of veins—

Melted now, the wings regrow within me,
only now, wings lost, do I feel them true;
and to reckless hearts I cry, *"mortals,*
passion is too important a ghost to be made flesh."

Full-maned, wandering Halley's comets, omens,
disasters, marvels that inflame and freeze our blood,
let no one dare bind you, let no one risk touching
clots of pure remoteness—meteors

(Beverly Allen)

IL DESTINO

Fu allora che il destino mi volle prendere per mano,
da questo istante, disse, la tua bianca esistenza
in me si fonde, assume una forma mai vista—
da questo istante intuisci l'infinito dei cieli.

Decifrare dei rebus è stata la tua vita,
eccoti ora la chiave, un solo sole t'illumina,
guarda di che colore si sono fatti i fiori
quando alle tue pupille io solo ho detto *apritevi* —

La morte è un radicale mozzafiato
ma ti è dato di scorgere il rovescio della medaglia—
ti hanno detto, bambina, che Dio è in ogni cosa
ed era un puro apologo, sinonimo di poesia—

Sei stata imprigionata in un castello di nebbie
con la mente allo stadio di pipistrello cieco—
ora cammina, alzati, ti dico. Prima di te l'ho detto
a Euridice, a Lazzaro, a ogni primavera stregata.

(1986)

MARIA LUISA SPAZIANI

DESTINY

It was then that destiny decided to take me by the hand,
from this moment on, destiny said, your empty existence
will melt into me, will take on a form never seen;
from this moment on, you will sense the infinity of the skies.

Deciphering puzzles has been your life,
here, now, is the key, one sun alone illuminates you,
look at the color the flowers have turned
since I said simply to your eyes, *open wide—*

Death really knocks the wind out of you
but it is given you to make out the other side of the coin—
they told you when you were a little girl that God is in all
     things
and it was pure apology, a synonym for poetry.

You've been locked in a castle of fogs,
your mind at the blind-bat stage—
now walk, arise, I say to you. Before you, I said it
to Eurydice, to Lazarus, to every bewitched springtime.

(Beverly Allen)

IL DUOMO

Quando stavo a Milano il Duomo aveva trent'anni di meno,
valchiria folle marzo galoppava,
un cielo di struggente acquamarina
mi rideva in pupille di pochi ricordi.

Ragazzetta la quercia del collegio
stringevano sul cuore trenta cerchi di meno,
la torre Velasca brillava nuova di zecca
riflettendo tramonti da isole papuasiche.

Come un cero la linguetta di fuoco,
ogni guglia scalare reggeva il suo santo.
Li vedevo sorridere, con la mia vista d'aquila,
palpebrare e ripetermi di sì.

Sotto tre lune piene ruotanti tutte insieme
per me fioriva fitto sul sagrato
un prato di narcisi su cui danzava Rimbaud.
Avevo qualche aureola in più, nel marzo di Milano.

(1986)

MARIA LUISA SPAZIANI

THE DUOMO

When I lived in Milan the Duomo was thirty years younger,
March used to gallop along like a crazed Valkyrie,
a sky of thawing aquamarine
used to laugh into my eyes remembering little.

When I was a girl, the schoolyard oak
held thirty circles fewer to its heart,
the Velasca tower shined sparkling new,
reflecting Papuan-island sunsets.

As a candle holds its tongue of flame,
each craggy spire held its saint.
With my eagle eye I saw them smile,
blink, and tell me yes.

Beneath three full moons in joint rotation
there bloomed for me, thick on the churchyard pavement,
a field of narcissus where Rimbaud danced.
I had a halo or two more then, that March in Milan.

(Beverly Allen)

IL GRANELLO DI SABBIA

Il granello di sabbia, l'inizio del deserto.
La molecola d'acqua, l'inizio della vita.
Un domani un domani un domani un domani un domani,
il rosario sfilato da miliardi di mani.

Un domani si salda di notte con l'altro domani,
ventiquattr'ore nascere, espandersi e morire—
muore giovane, a volte inconsumato,
odalisca che presto sfiorisce
dimenticata dal pascià.

Tubi sempre più stretti di cannocchiale,
giorni e giorni che alla fine rientrano.
La lente sfiora appena fiumi comete e nuvole,
vessilli, fulmini, uccelli del paradiso.

Non è mai esistito, pare, al mondo,
un domani di cifra gemella di un altro domani.
Ma una schiera di ieri si gràmola e livella:
i grigi, incappucciati e non redenti
giorni spediti al macero.

(1986)

MARIA LUISA SPAZIANI

THE GRAIN OF SAND

The grain of sand, the beginning of the desert.
The molecule of water, the beginning of life.
A tomorrow a tomorrow a tomorrow a tomorrow a tomorrow
the rosary strung by millions of hands.

One tomorrow melds at night with another tomorrow,
twenty–four hours to be born, to grow, and to die—
it dies young, at times unfulfilled,
an odalisque who withers soon,
forgotten by the pasha.

Constantly narrowing telescope tubes,
days and days that at last come back.
The lens barely skims over rivers, comets and clouds,
banners, lightning bolts, birds of paradise.

Never has there been, it seems, in all the world
a tomorrow that matched another tomorrow.
But a throng of yesterdays that brakes and levels off:
grey, hooded, and unredeemed
days all sent to be scrapped.

(Beverly Allen)

MARIA LUISA SPAZIANI

da LA STELLA DEL LIBERO ARBITZIO

VI

Viaggiare con troppi bagagli non è buona regola.
Ci sono cose che farai bene a reprimere,
velare, censurare, spingere giù nell'inconscio.
Operazione ovviamente da compiersi in tutta coscienza.

Esempio: hai rivisto anni dopo un ragazzo che amavi,
che allora era esile e biondo, geniale e gentile.
Lo sai: è per lui che di notte ti spogli sul ponte del Louvre.
Ma oggi lui ignora quanto con lui lo tradisci.

VII

Troverò in paradiso quel macilento tralcio di rosa
che a Mathausen fiorì dietro la baracca quattordici.
Avrà i suoi occhi ogni cosa capace di durare,
miracolata, innocente, ostinata e radiosa.

Troverò in paradiso la tua e la mia pazienza.
Ne faremo un collage con rendez-vous mancati,
e velieri arenati, e brandelli di scienza,
bandiere intrise di pianto, ostinate a sventolare.

MARIA LUISA SPAZIANI

from THE STAR OF FREE WILL

VI

Traveling with too much baggage is not a good idea.
There are things you'd do well to repress,
veil, censor, push down into your unconscious.
Obviously an operation to be performed quite consciously.

Example: years later you've run into a boy you used to love,
who at the time was slender, blond, clever, and kind.
You know it: it's for him you undress on the Louvre bridge
    at night.
But today he doesn't know how much you betray him
    with himself.

VII

I shall find in paradise that emaciated rose shoot
that bloomed at Mathausen behind barrack fourteen.
All things capable of enduring will look like that shoot,
all things miraculous, innocent, stubborn and shining.

I shall find in paradise your patience and my own.
Out of them, we'll make a collage with our missed rendezvous,
and sailboats run aground, and the shreds of science,
with flags soaked in tears, insisting on waving.

X

Domenica di provincia, querulo scampanio normanno
tra fronde che ritmano altissimo un tempo sfilacciato.
S'aprono il passo i falchi tra i fili della pioggia,
nembi neri incastonano un isoscele blu.

La pausa d'agosto lontana dai guai mediterranei
m'invita a infilare a ritroso le perle del passato.
Ho avuto quattro amori, inventato otto libri,
assorbito Vivaldi in certe sere di luna, —

Ho odiato il borghese che cauto rifugge da ogni estremo,
che in cambio d'equilibrio baratta l'anima e l'avventura,
ho visto che un cocker bastardo vale più di un amante
perché come tutti, ma onesto, sa offrirci quanto noi gli
    lanciamo.

(1986)

MARIA LUISA SPAZIANI

X

Sunday in the provinces, a plaintive Norman bell-peal
among fronds beating out a ragged tempo as loud as they can.
Hawks open up a pathway between threads of rain,
black clouds hold a blue triangle in their mounting.

August's pause far from Mediterranean woes
invites me to string backwards the pearls of the past.
I've had four loves, invented eight books,
soaked up Vivaldi on certain moonlit evenings—

I've despised the bourgeois who flees all extremes,
who barters soul and adventure for a little balance,
I've learned that a mongrel spaniel is better than a lover
because, like everyone else, he gives back what he gets,
  but honestly.

(Beverly Allen)

MARIA LUISA SPAZIANI

LA RIVA PIETOSA

Tu che rastremi in te ogni profondo
della mia mente-cuore,
che fai vergini e chiare le parole
quotidiane, le dracme corrose,
accogli le mie lettere: così
con la zattera è pietosa la riva.

Ti scriverò nei giorni fulgidissimi
e in giorni maledetti,
i giorni del cuore trionfante
e i giorni del cuore zitto
quando striscia e ci inchioda quel sospetto:
Tutto è già stato scritto?

(1987)

MARIA LUISA SPAZIANI

THE MERCIFUL SHORE

You who draw into yourself each depth
of my mind-heart,
you who make virginal and clear
everyday words, rusted drachmas,
accept my letters: thus
the shore is merciful to the raft.

I'll write to you on the most radiant days
and on the cursed days,
on days when the heart is triumphant
and on days when the heart is mute,
when that suspicion slithers up and nails us:
Has everything already been written?

(Beverly Allen)

EGEO

Dal principio del mondo dura questa musica.
Nacque fra acque un sasso,
chiacchieravano ondine in morbido esperanto.
Non avrebbe previsto la chitarra
un guscio di testuggine marina.
Da sempre sale al cielo la tua musica,
verde radice prima, mamma-mare,
prima di tutti i prima. Ci avviluppi
nutrendoci di musica—minaccia,
favola, ipnosi, ninnananna, rombo,
presagio, mito,
               piccole agonie
di graniglie, relitti, di allegrie—

(1987)

MARIA LUISA SPAZIANI

THE AEGEAN

This music has lasted since the world began.
A rock was born among the waters
while tiny waves chatted in a soft universal tongue.
The shell of a sea-turtle
would not likely have foretold the guitar.
Your music has always risen to the sky,
green taproot, Mother Sea,
first of all firsts. You enfold us,
nurturing us with music—threat,
fable, hypnosis, lullabye, roar,
omen, myth,
              little agonies
of grit, of wreckages, of joys—

(Beverly Allen)

ROSSANA OMBRES

ROSSANA OMBRES

CRITICAL NOTE

Rossana Ombres, born in Turin in 1931, has had an active and wide-ranging career. For years the literary critic of the influential Turin daily *La Stampa,* she has contributed poems, short stories, and articles to a number of well-known periodicals, including *Botteghe Oscure,* and has also written radio dramas. Her own work has been translated into a number of other languages. Her first novel, *Principessa Giacinta,* appeared in 1970 to general critical acclaim. Two other novels have followed. Beginning in 1956, she has published five volumes of poetry. Of these the most important, the centerpiece of her poetic career, is the 1974 volume *Bestiario d'amore* (Love's Bestiary). It won the coveted Premio Viareggio, and selections from it have been the most widely reprinted and translated of her works. Although the frequency of her publication has diminished in recent years, the latest poems included here, which were published in 1988, demonstate the continuing quality of her work. She currently lives in Rome.

The earliest selection included here, the two-part "Excursion to Ravenna," is written in a compressed and allusive style. Presenting vividly sketched scenes and personalities, it reflects the influence of novelistic stream-of-consciousness technique. The young girl Angela absorbs impressions and experiences and keeps her feelings to herself, but the poem's ironic juxtapositions unmistakably communicate her reactions. The poems from *Bestiario d'amore*, by contrast, are written in a more open, narrative mode that often combines familiar Biblical events with unusual elements of Talmudic lore, all held in suspension by the unique sensibility of the poet. This style resurfaces in her latest work in the grimly fanciful "Strange Adventure." The other two new poems, briefer and more sharply etched, display the same inquisitive and quizzical approach that has always informed her poetry.

—M.P.

POETRY

Orizzante anche tu. Florence, 1956.
Le ciminiere di Casale. Milan, 1962.
L'ipotesi di Agar. Turin, 1968.
Bestiario d'amore. Milan, 1974.
Orfeo che amo Orfeo (in *Almanacco dello
    Specchio*, n.4). Milan, 1975.

OTHER

Principessa Giacinta (novel). Milan, 1970.
Le belle statuine (opera). Turin, 1975.
Memorie d'una dilettante (novel). Milan, 1977.
Serenata (novel). Milan. 1980.

GITA A RAVENNA
DI UNA BAMBINA COI SUOI GENITORI

ORE DEL MATTINO

Ci vuole la sabbia del mare, lo sappiamo
da tempo, la sabbia—ha detto—bianca
(le piacciono i colori sporchi presto);
la mamma dice: d'oro.

Buttare male la gamba sinistra avere,
diciamo empiricamente, l'anca strabica;
il padre sostiene
è sacrosanto il fattore ereditario
nel mondo che lui pensa
il padre pensa alla pulizia delle donne
gru oleate che portano in bilico la merce,
non fu marinaio
per via della vista.

Angela conosce il bianco colore che si sporca
la puzza d'anestetico il lampone dentro la bocca
i camici delle Balene Bianche da drizzare
        la gamba indolenzita
l'illustre clinico
che parla del mare come dell'olio di ricino: Angela

E X C U R S I O N   T O   R A V E N N A
O F   A   Y O U N G   G I R L   W I T H   H E R   P A R E N T S

MORNING HOURS

One needs sand from the sea, we have known
for some time, the white sand, he said
(she likes colors quickly soiled);
mother said: golden.

To sling in the left leg, to have,
we say empirically, a wild hip;
father maintains
the hereditary factor is sacrosanct
in a world that he thinks
father thinks of the purity of women
greased cranes that carry merchandise in their balance,
he had not become a sailor
because of his eyesight.

Angela knows the white color that becomes soiled
the stench of anesthetic the raspberry in the mouth
the uniforms of the White Whales for straightening
    the aching leg
the illustrious physician
who speaks of the sea as of castor oil: Angela

vorrebbe che
—paletta odore gomma scarafaggi viola
cose molli e scivolose—
per favore, non si facessero confusioni.

(1962)

ORE DEL POMERIGGIO

Tra le colombe a bere, Galla Placidia,
dove finiscono le calzette, il fresco
comune delle grotte, a sedere a provare il buon tempo...
Il selciato appena innaffiato
—dice il padre—può far salire il bacillo
del paratifo, e anche l'anguria per questo
anche la conchiglia che si succhia il mollusco col callo
pulite devono essere le donne
l'infezione del mondo è avvolta in chiffon
(non fu medico perchè rimetteva
in sala anatomica).

La chiesa grande nel prato la chioccia
tocchi le piume diritte e sporgono
vergini imbalsamate, piangono

ROSSANA OMBRES

would like that
—shovel odor rubber roaches purple
things damp and slippery—
they please not create confusion.

(Robert McCracken and Pietro Pedace)

AFTERNOON HOURS

Among the drinking doves, Galla Placidia,
where the ankle-socks end, the grottoes'
common coolness, sitting enjoying the moment...
The pavement barely sprinkled,
father says, can bring out the paratyphoid
bacillus, and also watermelon for that matter
as well as the shell that you suck out the mollusk
      with the foot
women must be kept pure
the world's infection is wrapped in chiffon
(he had not become a doctor because he threw up
in anatomy class).

The big church in the meadow the hen
you touch the hard feathers and embalmed virgins
rise, the watermelons

le angurie con tutti i semi,
un cosciente citofono tuona all'interno:
«Peccato è peccato
stare soli e senze più semi,»
Annaspano i crocifissi
e le farfalle della zia Bettina di Buenos Aires
puntati con lo spillo penduli d'un colore sporcabile
Apollinare
«in classe,» e ritorna la voglia del quaderno
mosso alla pagina dell'icona,
(la cresima è bella a Vienna, Angela,
che infiorano le macchine di piume)
«Teodorico—domani, nel toccarsi
la bolla di calore—aveva un bagno rosso.»

(1968)

weep with all their seeds,
a conscious earphone blares inside:
"It is a sin
that they're left alone with no more seed."
The crucifixes flail
and the butterflies of Aunt Bettina from Buenos Aires
pierced with a pin dangling a soilable color
Apollinare
"in Classe," and the desire for the notebook returns
opened tothe icon's page,
(Confirmations are beautiful in Vienna, Angela,
they decorate their cars with feathers)
"Theodoric," tomorrow, while touching her
fever sore, "had a red bath."

(Robert McCracken and Pietro Pedace)

CIMICE PRATAIOLA

Aluqa, demone che nuota sott'acqua nei torrenti
e cerca di farsi bere
e di appiccicarsi ai piedi dei ragazzini e alle zampe
delle pacifiche bestie,
si è appiattato
fra l'alluce del piede destro d'un profeta
e la striscia di cuoio del suo sandalo.

Il profeta lo ha portato nel piede
vagando tra grassi e magri
fin quando non è arrivato
in mezzo alle stelle come stava scritto.
Il mezzo alle stelle è un luogo
dove le ginocchia non si stancano
e i vestiti non si sporcano.

Lì Aluqa fu subito snidato
per il suo colore: solo il demone dell'acqua
aveva un colore indietreggiante, il vile
colore dell'angoscia.

Quando ricadde in uno stagno, Aluqa
fu scambiato per una cimice di prato
e inghiottito da una vecchia rana.

(1974)

MEADOW BUG

Aluqa, the demon who swims underwater in streams,
tries to get swallowed by someone
and to stick to small boys' feet and to the paws
of peaceful animals,
concealed himself
between the prophet's right great toe
and the leather strip of his sandal.

The prophet carried him on his foot
wandering between fat and lean
until the time when he arrived
in the middle of the stars, as it was written.
The middle of the stars is a place
where your knees never get tired
and clothes never get soiled.

There Aluqa was immediately discovered
by his color: only the demon of water
had a receding color, the base
color of anguish.

When he fell back into a pond, Aluqa
was mistaken for a meadow bug
and swallowed by an old she-frog.

(Ruth Feldman)

I M B A L S A M A T O R E

C'è un imbalsamatore che opera
con una forcina di Madonna Gioconda:
al posto del sangue e dei gangli nervosi,
nei sacchetti di arteria asciugata,
mette trina di mussola e spugna marina e segatura d'ossa
della puttana Maddalena.

Con l'intestino conciato della marmotta dà i punti.
Si fa accompagnare da un cane cieco.
E da un pappagallo che balbetta scuse per i parenti
del festeggiato.

Oggi tenterà la sua imbalsamazione quotidiana
con una creatura gentile che si chiama Eleazar:
re e governatori hanno seguito Eleazar
senza ch'egli mai usasse
radici di genipa o foglie di lauro
e oggi Eleazar invocherà Avzhia, angelo della presenza.

Il cane già punta gli occhi putrefatti
dove gli par di sentir sgrovigliarsi da un cespuglio
un gigantesco usignolo.

(1974)

EMBALMER

There is an embalmer who operates
with one of Madonna Gioconda's hairpins;
in place of blood and nerve ganglions,
in the small sacs of dried-up artery
he puts muslin lace, sea-sponge and sawdust of bones
of the harlot Magdalen.

He uses tanned marmot-gut for stitches.
He is accompanied by a blind dog.
And by a parrot that stammers apologies for the relatives
of the one who's being fêted.

Today he will attempt his daily embalming
with a nice creature called Eleazar:
kings and governors have followed Eleazar
without his ever having used
madder roots or laurel leaves
and today Eleazar will invoke Avzhia, angel of presence.

The dog already turns its putrefied eyes
to where it thinks it hears a giant nightingale
extricate itself from a thicket.

(Ruth Feldman)

FIORE ACCALAPPIATORE DI SALMI

C'è un fiore che fiorisce fuori stagione
e somiglia
per la sua conformazione
ad un asso di spade:
ha il colore di una lama e lancinante
è quel suo profumo di nemesi.

Ha un talamo debordante
che mugola di risentimento o d'amore,
gonfio e vivamente colorato
come l'impugnatura di un asso di spade.

Lo sognò, una notte,
un profeta
e
lo vide al mattino:
mugolava forte
vicino alla porta di casa
piantato in un mucchietto di terra tremante
come la groppa d'un cavallino in corsa.

ROSSANA OMBRES

ENSNARING FLOWER OF PSALMS

There is a flower that blooms out of season
and in its form
resembles
an ace of swords:
it's the color of a blade and its perfume,
that of Nemesis, stabs you.

It has an overflowing thalamus
that howls with resentment or with love,
swollen and brightly colored
like the hilt of an ace of swords.

A prophet
dreamed about it one night
and
saw it in the morning:
it was howling loudly
near the house-door, stuck into a little heap
of quivering earth
like the rump of a running colt.

ROSSANA OMBRES

A pochi è dato di vedere
il fiore accalappiatore di salmi
che fiorisce quando il tempo dei fiori
è distante e dimenticato:
e solo i più santi
lo sentono gemere.

(1974)

ROSSANA OMBRES

It is given to very few to see
the ensnaring flower of Psalms
that blooms when the time of flowers
is far off and forgotten:
and only the most godly people
hear it moan.

(Ruth Feldman)

BALLATA DELLA FIGLIA DI NOÈ

Fu prima a toccare la terra la figlia di Noè
(gli altri temevano
che qualche inopportuna deità paludale
esigesse lo scialo d'un sacrificio umano)
e nella insicura sostanza
di germi effervescenti
lei camminava
ancora non completamente
sottratta al sogno.

...e apparve un grande chigio tappezzato
di squame cruciverbiche, e in un fiume
che si restringeva grinzandosi
due folaghe diedero un amoroso salto maculato.
Cento bernache lasciarono in volo
le loro conchiglie
che il mare aveva spinto in una secca.
S'affacciò la rana ammantata di sabbia, vorace
delle piccole prede che la quiete
aveva rincuorato; e una trota
dall'ovaio congestionato
cavalcò un mulinello
del lago ch'era già tutto rientrato nel suo stampo.

BALLAD OF NOAH'S DAUGHTER

The first person to set foot on land was Noah's daughter
(the others were afraid
that some inopportune bog god
might require the heavy cost of a human sacrifice)
and in the unsteady substance
of effervescent seeds
she kept walking,
still not entirely
delivered from her dream.

...and a big serpent appeared, sheathed
in crossword scales, and in a stream
that narrowed, rippling,
two perch gave an amorous dappled leap.
A hundred plant-ducklings took flight,
leaving behind their shells
that the sea had pushed onto a sandbank.
The sandcloaked frog appeared, ravenous
for small prey that the quiet
had emboldened, and a trout
with its swollen egg-case
bestrode a whirlpool of the lake
already refilling its mold completely.

Un lungo vagito
annunciò la presenza
dell'Angelo dei Cominciamenti.

Nell'arca, intanto,
un tumulto d'euforia: l'ultima botte
è rovistata fin dentro le sue placente;
il gallo insegna
quanto è volgare e stridula la morte della notte.
Nel baldorioso sabba d'animali
si confondono grevi specie e sesso
e un vergognoso fiato
è l'incenso dello stravolto altare...

Ma ormai
il primo cespo di palme asciutto
è pronto a soccorrere creatura che voli
obelischi di vittoria sono riemerse le montagne
e risplendono sull'affanno delle distese d'acqua in fuga.
Lontano dal corrotto tanfo dell'arca
la figlia di Noè
rabbrividisce appena ai nuovi aromi:
né l'olivo lassù, a braccia aperte,
la intenerisce;
gli altri

ROSSANA OMBRES

A lengthy wail
announced the presence
of the Angel of Beginnings.

In the Ark, meanwhile,
a tumult of revelry: the last cask
is ransacked right down to its placentas;
the cock teaches
how vulgar and strident is the death of night.
In the riotous Animals' Sabbath
burdensome species and sex are mixed
and the incense of the sacrilegious altar
is a shameful breath...

But by now
the first tuft of dried palm trees
is ready to succor any flying creatures;
obelisks of victory, the mountains have resurfaced
and they shine on the troubled expanses of receding water.
Far from the Ark's polluted stench
Noah's daughter
hardly shivers in the new aromas:
nor does the olive tree with open arms high above
move her;
the others

quelli del barcone che ora naviga sabbia
gli uomini le bestie
sono in festa: e ciò che s'ode
non si sa se è nitrito o lamento di troia che
    sgrava
o risata d'ubbriachezza
non si sa se è ringhio o furore di lite o foia
di un coito immondo. Neppure si sa
se chi abita l'arca
ha voglia di restarvi prigioniero
o convertito a un nume capriccioso (che chiede
in cambio della libertà
l'estinzione di una specie sgradita)
cerchi d'acquetarlo con l'inganno.

Intanto lei
la figlia di Noè
sorveglia l'apprensione
dello scoglio che preme come un feto maturo
e nella bassa marea schizza fuori,
guarda una galleria di roccia
che svuotandosi diventa cattedrale.
Lei sa
che se fanno festa nell'arca, ebbene
festa non è:

the ones of the big boat now navigating sand
the men the beasts
are celebrating: and you can't tell
whether what you hear is a whinny
or the squeals of a sow giving birth, or drunken laughter;
you don't know if it's a snarl or the fury of a quarrel or
    the rut
of an unclean coupling. You don't even know
if those who inhabit the Ark
would like to stay prisoners
or having converted to a capricious deity (who demands
in exchange for liberty
the extinction of an undesirable species),
they are seeking to appease him with deceit.

Meanwhile she,
the daughter of Noah
watches over the anxiety
of the rock that presses like a mature foetus
and spurts out in the low tide,
she looks at a gallery of rock
that, emptying itself, becomes a cathedral.
She knows
they're celebrating in the Ark, and yet
it's not a celebration:

distante è ancora il giorno del gran sole
(la figlia di Noè
qualche volta parlò, mentre cuoceva
focacce, con un cherubino itinerante)
quando saranno lette le parole sante
lontano il banchetto della gioia
quando si mangerà polpa di leviatano.
L'angelo dalle ali di gabbiano
—che guida con i suoi vagiti
ogni cominciamento—
s'appresta a suonare l'olifante.

(1974)

the day of the great sun is still far off
(while she was baking flatbread,
Noah's daughter spoke at times
to a wandering cherub)
when the holy words shall be read,
far off the banquet of joy
when the flesh of Leviathan shall be eaten.
The angel with seagulls' wings
—that with its wailing leads
every beginning—
gets ready to blow the oliphant.

(Ruth Feldman)

STRANA AVVENTURA

Da bambino (in Australia)
lo costrinsero a mangiare un canguro
appena nato—pesava
poco più di una quaglia.
Quando più tardi
glielo fecero ricordare
pensò d'essere diventato
un eroe fortunato.
Con questo suo incarnito
congiunto, i diffidenti demoni
avrebbero perso le loro dominazioni.
Col suo complice, il bere dei nemici
sarebbe stato secco ed il mangiare
pungicante. Avrebbe
vinto sempre
saltando ogni tappa
portando l'amico delle sue viscere
su labari ed else...

Scelse una vita
senza battaglie. Ma ogni notte
lotta con un animale
di una specie stravolta,

STRANGE ADVENTURE

As a child (in Australia)
he was forced to eat a newborn
kangaroo—it weighed
little more than a quail.
When, later on,
they made him remember,
he thought he had become
a lucky hero.
With this ingrown relative of his,
the distrustful demons
would lose their domination.
With his accomplice, the enemies' drinks
would be dry, the food
stinging. He would always
win,
leaping every lap
carrying the friend of his vitals
over banners and sword-hilts.

He chose a life
without battles. But every night
he wrestles with an animal

per tante stagioni cresciuto
in simbiosi con un umano:
che tenta d'immergerlo
in una palude marsupiale.
Ogni notte l'animale
con due estenuate brevi zampe davanti
lo prega, e con due giganti zampe dietro
lo destina a una brutale rovina.
Ogni mattina si sveglia più opaco
scialacquato dal sonno come
se la vita lo stesse tralasciando:
non vorrebbe che la lotta avesse fine
senza un segno senza una ferita.

(1988)

of a distorted species,
grown for so many seasons
in symbiosis with a human being:
who tries to immerse it
in a marsupial marsh.
Every night the animal
with two diminutive front legs
begs him, and with two huge rear ones
destines him to brutal ruin.
Every morning he wakes up duller,
wasted by sleep as though
life were leaving him behind:
he wouldn't like the struggle to end
without a mark without a wound.

(Ruth Feldman)

ROSSANA OMBRES

D O D I C I

Nell'angolo di un negozio di fiori
c'era (non ne avevo mai visti prima)
un vaso di stelle alpine.
Le ho contate: dodici lazzari
alzati nel loro sudario grigio
su terra schiumosa.
Amorevolmente le ho guardate.
«Non sono morte—ho detto—
ma solo addormentate.»

(1988)

ROSSANA OMBRES

TWELVE

In the corner of a flower-shop
there was (I had never seen one before)
a vase of edelweiss.
I counted them: twelve Lazaruses
risen in their gray shroud
on frothy ground.
I looked at them lovingly.
"They're not dead," I said,
"they're only sleeping."

(Ruth Feldman)

CASA BIANCA

Casa bianca davanti al parco
arcigna con l'opulenza delle piante.
Casa con la sua prima
virtù di fortitudo
nella sua inabilità a crescere
(inclinata com'è ad essere solo radice)
netta casa a due piani
dal portoncino stretto che ricorda
per quali strettoie s'incanala la vita,
con quel miracoloso di preghiera esaudita
che solo può ostinarsi nella calce...

Da quella casa vidi uscire te
con un'incarnato sconosciuto
gli occhi voraci e come
nascosta nel passo una crudeltà
dissennata.
Dissi: «Si muove, ecco, vivo e cresciuto
di vita» e una persiana
sbatté violenta e nera a un vento che non c'era.

(1988)

A WHITE HOUSE

A white house in front of the park
sulking at the opulence of the plants.
A house with its first
virtue of fortitude
in its inability to grow
(inclined as it is to be only root)
a trim two-story house
with a narrow doorway that recalls
through which narrows life is channeled,
with that wonder of answered prayer
that only can persist in lime...

From that house I saw you come
with an unfamiliar complexion
voracious eyes and as if
hidden in your step a mad
cruelty.
I said, "There, he moves, alive and flush
with life" and a shutter
slammed violent and black at a wind that wasn't there.

(Robert McCracken and Pietro Pedace)

ROSSANA OMBRES

NOTES ON THE POEMS

From "Meadow Bug"

Aluqa
Also in other poems in this collection appear aquatic demons of marshy areas and demons who inhabit latrines. In the demonology of Talmudic folklore, one often finds allusions to demonic entities that hide, favoring dirty and marshy places.

From "The Ballad of Noah's Daughter"

Plant ducklings
According to Medieval legend, ducklings could grow on trees.

The sandcloaked frog
The predatory frog swathed in sand is described in Cicero's *De natura deorum*.

When the holy words shall be read
From a popular Yiddish song that tells of this future banquet.

When the flesh of Leviathan shall be eaten
From the aforesaid Yiddish song. References also exist to Islamic texts of Ishmaelite origin.

RODOLFO DI BIASIO

RODOLFO DI BIASIO

CRITICAL NOTE

Rodolfo Di Biasio, born in Ventosa in 1937, lives and works in Formia. Like most of his colleagues and contemporaries, he is involved in a wide range of literary activities. He has previously edited the journal *L'Argine letterario*, and is presently the editor of *Rapporti*, a quarterly. His reviews, articles, and contributions to symposia have appeared in numerous periodicals, and he writes for RAI (Radiotelevisione Italiana). He is also the editor of *Oltre il Novecento*, a series of monographs, with selections from their work, on contemporary Italian poets, and has himself written a volume in the *La Nuova Italia* series of critical texts. Di Biasio's poetry and fiction have appeared in literary journals and anthologies, both in Italy and abroad, and have been translated into a number of foreign languages. Beginning in 1962, he has at widely spaced intervals published four collections of carefully crafted verse, as well as two collections of fiction. Over the past twenty years, his work has gradually become the subject of extensive critical commentary.

Like Fabio Doplicher, with whom he has a close professional relationship, Di Biasio writes a poetry of austere surfaces in which, while the expression of emotion is strictly disciplined, its pressure can be felt just below the surface. Like Doplicher, he is essentially classical in perspective. He views the modern world as a bleak landscape of discrete components. Less thickly textured than Doplicher's, Di Biasio's work strives to achieve, however precariously, a unifying vision. The poems included here, which appear consecutively in his 1987 collection, *I ritorni* (*The Returns*), are very closely connected in theme and structure. In each, the title provides a center around which the poem's images and inquiries seek to cohere—as in "Nostoi," which outlines a voyage that is, if not so violent or tragic, still as errant and untriumphant as those of the Achaian heroes after the Trojan War. Each pursues in its three sections a journey through a waste land both personal and universal—as in "Poem of the Dawn and the Night," with its vigil for the vivifying rain, in which the fragments that we shore against our ruin are composed of "the defenseless word / doleful sign that consigns us to other hands / the few reaching out." However defenseless the words may be, the chiseled lines themselves communicate the stoic dignity that enables us to endure such a world.

—M.P.

POETRY
Niente è mutato. Padua, 1962.
Poesie dalla terra. Rome, 1972.
Le sorti tentate. Manduria, 1977.
I ritorni. Rome, 1986.

OTHER
Il pacco dall'America (fiction). Rome, 1977.
Bonaviri (criticism). Florence, 1978.
La strega di Pasqua (fiction). Foggia, 1978.

POEMETTO DELLA NEVE

I

Attendo notizie, me le porti
lo sciogliersi della neve
su questo bilanciato silenzio

Dei fatti: incanutiscono nella breve ora di luce
li brucia un sole imbaldanzito
e una deriva li allontana li spazia
e inzavorrati calano in buchi neri
questa interna trama della terra
che è poi il suo riprendersi
il soffio il fiato nostro

E di me:
non mi tornano i gesti
le parole stesse si sfiorano
si chiude il tempo e traccia un suo cerchio
dolorosamente
persegue un suo disegno, ambiguo,
dove l'occhio si sperde
la rosa di luce che varca mare e cielo
ed essa mi scancella anche altre voci

RODOLFO DI BIASIO

SNOW POEM

I

I am waiting for news, let it come
with the melting of the snow
on this even silence

Of the facts: they grizzle in light's brief hour
are burned by an emboldened sun
distanced, scattered by a driftage
and ballasted they fall into black holes
this inner weft of earth
which actually is only earth
catching its breath, our wind

And of myself:
the gestures do not come back to me
words themselves are just barely touched
time closes and traces its circle
sorrowfully
it follows a design of its own, ambiguous,
in which the eye gets lost
rose of light spanning sea and sky
obliterating other voices as well in me

RODOLFO DI BIASIO

le mie le vostre
perciò attendo notizie, un segno,
la spirale di fumo
i quieti rumori della casa

II

L'attesa s'affissa
allo sciogliersi della neve
che ripete il rito di primavera,
è l'orlo della vita
quando tornano alla terra i suoi colori
giallo e bianco
disseminati colori che l'occhio discopre
con meraviglia per noi ora
che forse nulla sappiamo
e non conosciamo

Dove il vento porta le nubi
o quando il sole taglia radente il verde delle querce
come sottilmente trama la terra il suo viaggio

Nella deriva gli anni accumulati
non colgono il responso:

RODOLFO DI BIASIO

my own your own
that's why I'm waiting for news, a sign,
the spiral of smoke
the quiet noises of the house

II

The wait is linked
to the melting of the snow
in repetition of spring's ritual
it's the edge of life
when earth's colors return
yellow and white
scattered colors the eye discovers
with wonder for us now
that we know perhaps nothing
have no idea

Where the wind carries the clouds
or when the sun cuts skimming the green of oaks
how subtly the earth plots its journey

In the driftage the accumulated years
do not grasp the oracle:

per routine Sibilla
disperde bizzarre capovolte foglie,
magri segni persistono
sillabazioni che non ci dismalano
che solo ci inducono a percorrere esili tracce,
l'infisso tragitto:
e non sappiamo se ospiti o figli
siamo destinati a durare

III

A questo punto solo resta
interrogare il già fatto:
ciglia filiformi capi?
Incunaboli
appena il sole chiude il suo corso
e la notte coniuga vicissitudini
l'intreccio persistente di tremori remoti

Poi che ancora? Scivola un'alba da poco
e i chiari suoni li disperde la luce

La memoria si gonfia d'acque
per un verde che incrina i dorsali,

RODOLFO DI BIASIO

by routine the Sybil
scatters overturned haphazard leaves,
meager signs persist
syllables that do not cure our ills
but only induce us to follow faint traces,
the unwavering path:
and we know not whether, guests or children,
we are destined to last

III

At this point all that remains
is to examine what's already happened:
eyelashes filiform heads?
Incunabula
as soon as the sun ends its course
and the night weds vicissitudes
the persistent weave of distant tremors

And what else still? a paltry dawn slips out
and bright sounds are scattered by light

Memory swells with waters
through a green that breaks up the crests,

spezza d'acchito il bianco, è ancora la neve,
e s'allarga in dimensioni astrali:
l'ombelico della vita
il dubbio
se siamo noi con le cose
o se camminiamo in cerca di che non sappiamo
il graffito dei giorni
che ingloba sole e azzurro
il fremito il guizzo del sangue
che si disfa in mondiglia

(1986)

shatters at once the whiteness, the snow again,
sprawling to astral dimensions:
life's umbilicus
doubt
whether we are with things
or we walk in search of what we don't know
the graffiti of the days
the quiver, the spurt of blood
that breaks down into dross

(Stephen Sartarelli)

P O E M E T T O   D E L L ' A L B A
E   D E L L A   N O T T E

I

Per una notte—qualsiasi—che si curva
o solo per una quercia
nella sua ombra agonica
verso—contro—stelle consuetudinarie
si scrive
            accade ancora di scrivere
il fermo della persiana
è il *flatus vocis*
che si stampiglia sul margine
dove le parole debordano
                non scritte non dette
l'inerme parola
il doloroso segno che ci consegna ad altre mani
le poche che si tendono

Poi un'alba colta per caso
nel battito di un'imposta
da una voce che più non conosci
                e dovresti
la terrena voce—la dolente—
se dentro perdurano reliquie

RODOLFO DI BIASIO

POEM OF THE DAWN AND THE NIGHT

I

For a night—any night—that bends
or only for an oak
in its agonic shade
toward—against—customary stars
one writes
            happens again to write
the latch of the window-blind
is the *flatus vocis*
stamped in the margin
where words overflow
                unwritten unsaid
the defenseless word
doleful sign that consigns us to other hands
the few reaching out

Then a dawn seized by chance
in the beating of a shutter
by a voice you know no more
                and should
the earthly voice—the sorrowful one—
if inside there still are relics

RODOLFO DI BIASIO

di cose di persone
le stesse che hanno scandito pulsioni indecifrabili
tremori—i tremori che la notte asseconda—
e il teporeodore di donna accanto
ancora lei ti fascia ed ora e sempre
quando si cangia in luce stellare
l'intera luce delle stelle

Un margine—è ora il margine dell'alba—
e l'evento non è che un'altra attesa
nell'esorcismo di albe e di notti
di altre albe di altre notti
consuetudinarie come le stelle
e poi la quercia che oppone
la sua ombra agonica

noi le inermi parole
noi inermi la parola

II

Sopravviene il giorno con il suo grido
l'espansione delle strade
i doloranti impegnidisimpegni

RODOLFO DI BIASIO

of things and people
the same that beat in enigmatic throbs
tremors—tremors echoed by the night—
and a scented warmth of woman beside you
again she envelops you now and forever
when she changes into astral light
all the light of the stars

A margin—it's now the dawn's margin—
and the event is only another wait
in the exorcism of dawns and nights
of other dawns and other nights
as customary as the stars
and the oak that imposes
its agonic shade

we the defenseless words
we defenseless, the word

II

The day arrives with its cry
the swelling of the streets
the painful engagements-disengagements

RODOLFO DI BIASIO

le cose le cose che fanno ressa
nemmeno il sortilegio del mare
scardina l'agrore di dentro
                la fittile spina
che la parola la mia la vostra
—è ancora l'inerme parola—
smuove per abitudine
nell'arco luminoso del sole
quando Capricorno si piega
e trema da ultimo sulle foglie

La bottiglia non porta il manoscritto
la parola di là dal mare
che dica lo sciogliersi della neve
anche il deserto
o il battito fraterno del cuore
se cattura nel pugno un attimo del tempo

la sua gloria il suo amore

III

O per l'attesa di un oltre:
ora che un cerchio d'ombra ci chiude, pare,
e il vuoto stellare ribadito dal vento

RODOLFO DI BIASIO

things and things that throng together
not even the sea's sorcery
can unhinge the bitterness inside
                    the clay thorn
that the word, mine and yours
—and still defenseless—
removes out of habit
in the sun's luminous arc
when Capricorn yields
and trembles at last on the leaves

The bottle contains no manuscript
no word from across the sea
that speaks of the snow's melting
even the desert
or the heart's fraternal beating
when it captures an instant of time

its glory, its love

III

O to wait for a beyond:
now that a circle of shadow surrounds us, it seems,
and the astral void, reinforced by the wind,

RODOLFO DI BIASIO

ci riporta nell'eguale deserto
e spia la pioggia
la sola che possa sciogliere
il torpido sangue

(1986)

takes us back to the same desert
and watches for rain
the only rain that might dissolve
the languid blood

(Stephen Sartarelli)

RODOLFO DI BIASIO

CUNCTA SEMPER

I

Si sfilano ancora
per una fibrillazione del sangue
le ceneri della parola calde
tramano poche faville il filo grigio
che la mano persegue
il guizzo e null'altro

Cuncta semper: certo...
ma chissà dove esse si dispongono
in un luogo di immobili querce
per un cielo che è fermo più fermo
della curvatura del tempo
azzurro il tempo fino allo spasimo
e curvo là dove il discrimine
confonde vento e profumi
e le nostre minute carovane non approdano
vinte come sono dal deserto
della consuetudine

Dentro... *cuncta semper*... certo...
un groviglio il più fondo

RODOLFO DI BIASIO

CUNCTA SEMPER

I

The warm ashes of the word
still come unravelled
from a fibrillation of the blood
a few sparks weave the grey thread
the hand follows
a flash and nothing more

Cuncta semper: of course...
but who knows where they settle
amidst immovable oaks
across a still sky more still
than time's bending
time blue to the point of agony
and bent where the crest
confuses wind and aromas
and our tiny caravans do not arrive
overcome as they are by the desert
of habit

Inside...*cuncta semper*... of course...
a tangle, the thickest

inestricabile grumo di eventi-parole
cenere calda cenere grigia
dove il gesto non interviene più
dove basterebbe la persuasione
d'essere stati vivi indispensabili
per un manipolo di giorni

II

Una tra le infinite polverose
distanza colmata finalmente
si slarga in questa abituale sortita di primavera
se soccorre l'occhio
e segue ad una ad una le ginestre
e poi come esse si fanno mare
che diseppellisce e ricuce
il giallo dondolio della montagna

Essa cerca per un'abitudine
sempre l'abitudine grigia
il suo luogo lo scorcio l'andito
il suo tempo anche

la perentoria consonanza
la stessa che richiede che è sua

RODOLFO DI BIASIO

indissoluble clot of words-events
warm ash grey ash
where the act no longer intervenes
where it would be enough to believe
we'd been alive and indispensible
for a handful of days

II

One among the endless dusty distances
one finally filled
opens out in this customary entrance of spring
if the eye comes to aid
and follows one by one the broomflowers
as they become a sea
that unearths and restitches
the yellow swaying of the mountain

The distance searches out of habit
always the same grey habit
for its place—prospect, passage—
and for its time

the peremptory consonance
the same that demands as its own

RODOLFO DI BIASIO

la ginestra al tempo di primavera
se il vento asseconda il soffio dell'erba
sotto il piede

La pozza di luce cancella
espansa folgore senza slabbrature
oh a quel punto
parrebbe eterna la luce e cancella tronca
gli avvolgimenti quei sottili avvolgimenti
che legano in un sottobosco di memorie
e ripropone il miracolo della ripetizione

III

Altra nebbia, quella viva delle incerte mattine
di maggio per la collina
quella che poi il sole scardina
ulivo dopo ulivo
e dissotterra il fiato della casa
altra nebbia ha pareggiato materiati gorghi
e li ha colmati di un suo respiro grigio
o l'inamovibile nebbia
questa volta della notte
dove le parole risultano echi
ramificazioni
essenze tenaci persistenti

RODOLFO DI BIASIO

the broom in springtime
when the wind seconds the grass's murmur
under the feet

The pool of light annuls
vast flash with no frayed edge
oh at that point
the light seems eternal and cuts short, annuls
the winding paths, the narrow paths
that meet in an underbrush of memories,
presents again the miracle of repetition

III

Another fog, the bright one of uncertain mornings
in May across the hill
the one the sun later takes apart
olive by olive
the one that exhumes the home's breath
another fog has levelled sudden eddies
and filled them with its grey exhaling
and the irremovable fog
of night this time
where words come out as echoes
ramifications
tenacious, persistent essences

RODOLFO DI BIASIO

Dove in ressa s'affannano i volti
dalla loro regione disabitata
il marmo dei volti
essi essi che chiedono gelidamente
il consenso
e ribadiscono
la particula del tempo
insieme consumata su strade usuali
screpolate strade ora
che non trattengono
un solo segno della loro persistenza

(1986)

RODOLFO DI BIASIO

Where faces in a throng toil breathless
from their deserted regions
the faces' marble
they, they who coldly ask
for permission
and reconfirm
time's particle
at once consumed along much-travelled roads
now crumbling roads
that do not retain
a single sign of their persistence.

(Stephen Sartarelli)

RODOLFO DI BIASIO

I NOSTOI

I

Dove—il luogo delle concatenazioni
è vero che primavera o autunno
coincidono ancora per flussi rigeneratori
o per apparenti morti—
i ritorni
i progettuali ritorni
che il vento o il sommovimento delle nubi
per il crinale bruciato dello strame
riscavano

Finalmente
il passo richiede la sua quiete
e l'occhio si infigge dove agiscono
le sottili e minute creature dell'aria
esperte del canto
o le altre della terra, anche il serpe
il giacinto spontaneo o l'erba o una viola di ciglio
le stesse
disimparate
per insensatezze di desiderio

NOSTOI

I

Where—the place of concatenations
it's true that spring and fall
still coincide in regenerative flux
or in apparent deaths—
the returns
the projected returns
that the wind or the stirring of the clouds
through the hay's blasted mane
exhumes

At last
the footstep demands its quiet
and the eye plunges deep to where
the tiny, slight creatures of the air
adepts of song
or those of the earth, even snakes
or the sudden hyacinth, the grass or a cliffhanging violet
move about, the very same
unlearned
through follies of desire

RODOLFO DI BIASIO

Il brodo caldo dell'esistere
risana come risana
le screpolature delle labbra
espande la sua sanità l'aroma dell'asprigno prunastro
e impazzisce il turbine dei pollini
l'umidore del vento

II

È notte, l'ora del ritorno, la crudele notte
del Carro che ribadisce solitudini stellari
il non senso dei nostri pochi tragitti
e tramano i neon
disperazione dissipazione
che la pietà dell'alba non colma
la pietosa luce la pietà della luce
non cancella gli attossicati pomi della notte
e le tenebre infinitamente trapassano i neon

Oh le corolle! il tremuoto delle corolle
se il vento della montagna
nasce per uno spasimo
e s'inerpica il desiderio

e sogna il cuore il sogno delle vastitudini

RODOLFO DI BIASIO

The hot broth of living
cures as it does
the chapping of lips
the scent of tart plumcot spreads its health
and the whirl of pollen runs wild
the moisture of the wind

II

It's night, the moment of return, cruel night
of the Dipper clinching stellar solitudes
the nonsense of our few travels
while the neon lights weave
desperation dissipation
which the mercy of the sunrise cannot defeat
the merciful light, the mercy of light
does not annul the poison apples of the night
as shadows endlessly transfix the neon

And the corollas! their tremor
when the mountain wind
rises in a spasm
and desire begins to climb

and the heart dreams the dream of vastnesses

L'isola felice
ad essa è negato—ancora—il ritorno
e le usuali storie le prime
                              già Espero trama
solitudini

III

Si gonfia il desiderio del mare
ricerca smarrite peripezie
simmetrie
i lidi concavi di luna
precipizi
la rotta infissa dell'Olandese
nutre amore disamore
è il solo ormai solo
conosce la piegatura della Croce del Sud
quando l'equatore ruota
e maree prolungano il moto delle stelle
le desolate anabasi del desiderio

Il suo ritorno smagrisce:
accensioni e spegnimenti del polo
incidono rughe sul mare

RODOLFO DI BIASIO

The happy island
there return is denied—still—
as are the customary stories
the first ones
                    already Hesperus is weaving
solitudes

III

The sea's desire swells
it seeks lost recognitions
symmetries
the concave moonshores
precipices
the Dutchman's charted course
harbors love unloving
the lone one left alone
it knows how the Southern Cross bends
when the equator turns
and tides extend the motion of the stars
the desolate anabases of desire

Its return depletes:
the firmament's flashings and fadings
cut furrows in the sea

RODOLFO DI BIASIO

si corrispondono le bianche aurore vermiglie
i bianchi del ghiaccio
e l'ossessione dell'eterno ritorno
in un navigare senza remo

(1986)

RODOLFO DI BIASIO

the white vermilion daybreaks
the whites of the ice
the obsession of eternal return
correspond in oarless navigation

(Stephen Sartarelli)

NOTES ON THE POEMS

From "Cuncta semper"

Cuncta semper means "all things taken together."

From "Nostoi"

Nostoi is the title of a lost poem of the Epic Cycle describing the adventures of various heroes on their return home from the Trojan War. The word means the "returns" or "homecomings."

FABIO DOPLICHER

FABIO DOPLICHER

CRITICAL NOTE

Born in Trieste in 1938, Fabio Doplicher lives in Rome, where he is a visible presence on the contemporary poetry scene. One of the founders of the Centro Internazionale Poesia della Metamorfosi in Fano, he has used that organization to challenge many of the current assumptions of Italian poetry as well as introduce foreign poetry to the Italian audience. Doplicher also founded and originally edited the review STILB, and continues to direct the review's publishing operations. He has read from his poetry or lectured not only in Italy, but in France, Spain, Greece, Bulgaria, the Soviet Union, the United States, and elsewhere. He has edited several anthologies, including *Il pensiero, il corpo*, a 1986 selection of Italian poetry of the previous twenty years (with Umberto Piersanti) and *Il teatro dei poeti*, a collection of dramatic works by poets (1987). He himself has written a number of works for the theater, radio, and television, several of which have been produced by leading Italian directors. Over the past twenty years, he has published seven volumes of poetry. His work has been translated into fifteen languages.

With their long lines, solid stanzas, and extended length, even in their appearance on the page Doplicher's poems suggest the difficult and often demanding quality of his work. Images and metaphors come in thick, compressed clusters, as the poems move forward through associational leaps. Doplicher's poems frequently alternate between repulsion for the modern world and gentle longing for a purer existence. Like Matthew Arnold, Doplicher sees poetry as a spiritual critique of modern culture. Faced with a post-industrial wasteland, Doplicher muses the difficult necessity of personal relationships in a disconnected and eroded world, an environment in which "a philosophical body, contending with time,/attends to itself, disguised with sexton's grease-paint. the soul/inhabits the void, looks at it in laughter ..." The late Italian poet Giorgio Caproni pointed out that "Doplicher entitled one poem 'The Wish to Sing,' as if lyricism were a need in continual conflict with our time." Caproni also described the landscape of Doplicher's poetry as "a mental panorama in which emotionalism united with the hardness of images is in perpetual conflict with reason ..." Out of these and other conflicts (such as between the inescapable reality of things and the "need not to have been born"), Doplicher has fashioned a substantial body of work that in its intellectual seriousness rivals the work of any of his contemporaries.

—M.P.

POETRY

Il girochiuso. Rome, 1970.

La stanza del ghiaccio. Rome, 1971.

I giorni dell'esilio. Manduria, 1975.

La notte degli attori. Rome, 1980.

Le masque de Faust. Brescia-Paris, 1981.

La rappresentazione. Rome, 1984.

Curvano echi dentro l'universo. Foggia, 1985.

L'edera a Villa Pamphili. Bergamo, 1989.

Sonetti di Kiev. S. Benedetto del Tronto, 1989.

OTHER

Poesia della Metamorfosi, Rome, 1984.

L'ESILIO INCOMPLETO

Una tregua densa oggi tu sei, mia coccinella, èlitre rosse
per guance, sette punti neri le stelle
d'una scommessa perduta. A centinaia abbassano ora
la ramazza quotidiana come una coda monca, uomini
     camminando
sui propri sputi. Nella sotto-Roma, cattedrale del lurido
che fa altarini ai crocicchi, il vecchio impazzito
nero controsole predica con un foglio in mano,
sbavando. Combatti, immaginazione, ti sgretoli come
     l'intonaco
alle finestre che fiaccolano il sole di questo bordello. E festa,
è tanta festa, le sporche grinze del ben vivere fra piega e
     piega
si dipanano in vetrina. Un intermezzo, coccinella,
     imbòccati,
deponiamo qui l'anima: ci copriranno i rampicanti
dei tristi condomìni che nascondono le malattie del cemento.

Questo mediocre bisogno di non essere nato, cara, una
     scorciatoia,
viottolo fra lamiere al sole, che il demolitore stiva:

FABIO DOPLICHER

UNFINISHED EXILE

You're a teeming truce today, my ladybug, red elytra
for cheeks, seven black dots the stars
of a lost wager. In hundreds now they lower
the daily broom like a docked tail, men walking
in their own spit. In Rome's netherworld, cathedral of filth
that builds little altars at the crossroads, the old madman
black against the sun preaches with a sheet in hand,
slavering. You fight, imagination, crumble like the plaster
round the windows that torch this brothel's sun. It's a holiday,
so much a holiday, the dirty wrinkles of good living
    between the folds
unravel in shop windows. An intermission, ladybug,
    feed yourself,
let's lay down our souls here: we'll let ourselves be covered
    by the creeping
vines of sorry condominiums, which hide the diseases
    of the cement.

This mediocre need not to have been born, my dear, a shortcut,
footpath through scrap metal in the sun, stowed there
    by the wrecker:

le auto morte e i funerali di città sembrano cuccioli
    abbandonati.
Rassègnati, la vita sta qui, con la sua falda di cartone, eretta
in attesa. Le erbe e le alghe, i boschi di pini e i grandi
animali brucanti nei miei sogni di bambino
sono diventati petrolio. Una resa vile, nell'ombra dei
    vecchi quartieri
che espellono i poveri come il creatore scacciò la colpa
dal proprio edificio, e col carico grossolano di
    masserizie incongrue,
amalgamate di generazione in generazione, scendono
    le famiglie
per i gradini consunti, riscoprendoli uno per uno fin
    all'androne.

Di strato in strato compressi alle curvature dello
    stampo,
anima mia diventeremo cartone, ci aspetta un deposito
dove consumare questo tempo; ròso da un male segreto
    il gran pino
a Villa Pamphili ingiallisce rancido, le speranze,
    coccinella,
bruciano nere fumate nel conclave dei macellai che
    tagliano il nastro,
al traguardo di questo ciclo. Per me cominciò col mare

dead cars and city funerals seem like so many
   abandoned puppies.
Accept it, life is right here, with its layer of cardboard,
   upright
and waiting. The grasses and algae, the forests of pine and
the large animals grazing in my childhood dreams
have become petroleum. A cowardly surrender, in the
   shadow of old districts
that drive out the poor the way the creator expelled the sin
from his own edifice; and with the grotesque burden of
   household odds and ends
amassed down through the generations, families descend
the decrepit stairs, rediscovering them one by one all the
   way to the threshold.

From stratum to stratum compressed to the curves of
   the mould,
we shall, my soul, become cardboard, a depot awaits us,
where we may pass our time. Consumed by a secret illness
   the great pine
at Villa Pamphili turns yellow, rank, while hopes, my
   ladybug,
burn black smoke in a conclave of butchers who cut the
   tape
at this cycle's finish-line. For me it began with the sea

e con una tinozza di legno che faceva l'iride in odor
   di soda.
Sfaldiamo con le immagini di questa stagione a picco,
di pellicola in pellicola, ombra azzurrina sulla neve
   annuncia
una grande frana. Inferociti proliferano i frammenti che il
   verme acquatico
abbandonò nella pozza, sospesi e decomposti. A galla sopra
   un cimitero
di conchiglie svuotate, vedo i capelli di mio padre, di argento
   carico
in un guscio di madreperla, i suoi occhi fermi e ritrosi
quando un Natale di guerra ritornò con l'abete in mano.
   Lumini
diffusi fra aghi di pino il cancro, noi viviamo in un grande
   tumore.

Come i biancospini di Montebello, oggi accecati d'edifici
ho avuto la mia stagione di vento, l'amore in una famiglia
sono bòccioli bianchi vicini vicini, ma non è stata l'ultima
   bufera,
miei sogni sul mare, che al vento cedeva schiume salate
e i marinai americani come lanugini vetrose ai vicoli
   del porto.
Sono partito, coccinella, in un esilio incompleto, rose di
   plastica

FABIO DOPLICHER

and with a wooden tub that made the rainbow in a scent
    of soda.
We disintegrate together with the images of this headlong
    season,
from film to film, light blue shadow on the snow forbodes
a great landslide. Suspended piecemeal, the fragments the
    water-worm
left in the puddle multiply wildly. Floating above a
    graveyard
of empty conches, my father's hair appears, bright with
    silver
in a shell of mother-of-pearl, his eyes steady and wary
when he returned in war-time one Christmas with a fir-tree
    in his hand.
Small lamps scattered among pine-needles, cancer, we live
    inside a great tumor.

Like the whitethorns of Montebello, today blocked by
    buildings,
I have had my windy season, love in a family is like
white buds tightly huddled together, but it was not the
    last storm,
my dreams on the sea, which surrendered the briny foam to
    the wind
and the American sailors like glassy greenhorns to the alleys
    of the port.
I have left, ladybug, on an unfinished exile, plastic roses

ch'impòllinano ragnatele su una tomba, le ceneri della Risiera
in onde tenere come barba dei patriarchi inseguono l'oblìo,
esorbitante promessa, sui magici tappeti che i mercanti
    di Corfù
trafficavano nei fondaci, guizzando occhi lucidi fra
    le anticaglie.

A quest'ora nelle borgate svuotano buglioli, i giovani
    prigionieri
della oscura biscia, cisterne per acqua, cisterne per
    escrementi;
nella grande clinica del mondo, occhi di quarzo i medici
    del lager
sperimentano nuovi cristalli. La coscienza, una miccia
    fradicia
periodica scocca scintille alle ricorrenti fiamme.
    Ripetiamo
il ciclo distesi in anello, una catena di tenerezza
per cavalli senza fortuna al maneggio: a ponte
    Sisto ristagnano
rossi velami d'aria e l'àlito infetto dei pozzi artesiani
marci a pelo d'acqua, per le galere antiche

pollinating spiderwebs over a tomb, the ashes of la Risiera,
like the beards of patriarchs, pursue oblivion in soft waves,
exorbitant promise, on magic carpets that the merchants
    of Corfù
trafficked in streetshops, darting flashing eyes amid
    the antiques.

At this hour on the outskirts crappers are emptied by
    young prisoners
of the obscure snake, buckets for water, buckets for
    excrements;
in the great clinic of the world, eyes of quartz the
    prison-camp doctors
test new crystals. Conscience a wet fuse
intermittently shoots sparks at the recurrent flames.
    We repeat
the cycle, spread out in a ring, a chain of tenderness
for horses with no luck in riding: at the Sisto bridge
    red
veils of air grow stagnant, like the foul breath of
    artesian wells
rotten on the water's surface, through ancient galleys

dove ebrei pellegrini del rogo hanno recitato canzoni
     d'amore
e nenie sefardite. Pentiamoci, coccinella, la notte sfanga
limacciosa, cede alla luce sterpo dopo sterpo fra gli
     immondi
arbusti degli argini. Non ritroveremo il tempo
sospeso dentro le tue pupille, capricciose seguono
     un aereo
che irrora di odor cattivo l'universo fatale dei lotti
     fabbricati.

Come il burattinaio ubriaco esibisce ai passanti
la barba e l'ombelico, i pupazzi sparpagliati nei gesti
attoniti dei draghi e dei profeti, e le gengive dell'uomo fanno
     bolle
piccole bollicine e morde carta oleata, questa aurora ci ha
     compromessi
fra le sue quinte ammuffite, impregnati di disgusto e di pietà
con una moneta in mano, in mezzo alle comparse che
     s'affastellano al centro
nel rito deturpante del mattino. Questa lupa di Roma,
     coccinella,

FABIO DOPLICHER

where Jews, pilgrims of the stake, recited songs
    of love
and Sephardic laments. Let us repent, ladybug, the night
    emerges
slimy from the mud, surrenders to the light, twig after twig
    amid the filthy
shrubs on the banks. We shall not rediscover time
suspended in your eyes, as they whimsically follow an
    airplane
spraying foul odors on the fated universe of fabricated lots.

As the drunken puppetmaster shows passers-by
his beard and navel, and puppets scattered in astonished
acts of dragons and prophets, and the man's gums make
    bubbles
little bubbles as he bites wax-paper, so this dawn has
    compromised us
in its dusty side-scenes, soaked us with disgust and pity
as we hold a coin in hand, among the walk-ons jumbling
    at the center
in the disfiguring rite of morning. This Roman she-wolf,
    ladybug,

FABIO DOPLICHER

ha gli occhi dei pazzi e dei guardiani: vede la màcina al
    malleolo
nostro sporcato di catrame e i segni del tarlo che ingrana
    ogni notte
al respiro del mio sonno, con la fissità sospesa delle creature in
    gabbia
annoda come l'anima mia il proprio lenzuolo di nebbia.

(1975)

has the eyes of the insane and of watchmen: she sees the
    millstones on our malleoli
soiled with tar and the marks of the woodworm that meshes
    nightly
with the breath of my sleep, and with the frozen stillness
    of a creature in a cage
she knits, like my soul itself, her own blanket of fog.

(Stephen Sartarelli)

INTERREZZI
A Diderot

1.

su piazze calcinate bianchissime, i tori caricano
sciami inquietanti di vespe. la regione delle ipotesi
sospesa nell'anfiteatro tra infiniti gradini deserti.
amore, cosa potremmo essere, oggi che sappiamo
che qui non stiamo? il caso ha così deciso, l'automa
canta la storia del suo meccanismo perfetto,
impazzito all'altezza del cuore. lontano, sulla parete
di roccia ha costruito una tana il sentimento,
occhio d'aquila fissa l'infinita materia, il nostro
rigurgito della ragione, lattea cagliata orfana.
per dormire, il cuore cerca morbidi seni, la cantante
armonia del corpo eccita mostri, nella secca
della bassa marea palpita dentro la trincea di sabbia.

2.

di nervatura in nervatura, il baco da seta giura alle foglie

FABIO DOPLICHER

INTERLUDES
To Diderot

1.

in plazas calcined pure white, bulls charge
troublesome swarms of wasps. the realm of hypothesis
suspended in the amphitheatre amid endless empty tiers.
what could we be today, love, now that we know
we're not here? so has chance decided, the automaton
sings the story of its perfect mechanism
gone mad on a level with the heart. far away,
on a wall of stone, sentiment has built a nest,
eagle-eye stares hard at infinite matter, our
egestion of reason, orphaned milky curd.
to sleep, the heart seeks soft breasts, the body's
singing harmony rouses monsters. in the shallows
at low tide it palpitates inside a trench of sand.

2.

From nervation to nervation, the silkworm swears to the
        leaves

che per amore di vita le consuma. ma poi, nel bòzzolo, vomita
ridendo fili luminosi. bianca stella della ragione,
nodo dopo nodo il tuo viaggio si impiglia. oltre, la griglia
ferrea che perenne a questa ricerca spinge. indossata
la maschera, la tua seconda faccia diventa spiraglio
per lo spazio dilatante. perchè fingersi indifferenti,
    il nostro
cammino pesa. un corpo filosofo, che si confronta col
    tempo,
si cura, si traveste sotto il cerone del becchino. l'anima
abita il vuoto, lo guarda ridendo accoccolata nelle spirali
di madreperla. la polpa delle conchiglie fuggì, spaventata
per le lussuose escrescenze; e dentro il nulla, perpetua
    cerca
forme neutrali. un clavicembalo crea accordi colorati,
    amore.

3.

sensibili corde vibranti, quando l'indice blocca
una tastiera di sensazioni, diapason e silenzio.
nell'umido sotterraneo di un godere spento,
spifferi e sussurri, il secolo dei lumi si anima

FABIO DOPLICHER

that it's for life's sake that he consumes them. but later in the
   cocoon,
he vomits luminous threads, laughing. white star of reason,
knot after knot is your journey entangled. beyond, the iron
grid that forever spurs this quest. having donned
the mask, your second face becomes a narrow chink
for the widening space. why feign indifference? our
road weighs heavy. a philosophical body, contending
      with time,
attends to itself, disguised with sexton's grease-paint.
      the soul
inhabits the void, looks at it in laughter, squatting in spirals
of mother-of-pearl. the pulp of conch-shells has fled,
      frightened off
by luxuriant excrescences; and in nothingness it searches
      without end
for neutral forms. a harpsichord makes colored chords, love.

3.

sensible vibrating strings, when the forefinger blocks
a keyboard of sensations, diapason and silence.
in the humid basement of a now spent pleasure,
drafts and whispers, the age of enlightenment comes to life

nel raggio di una lucerna, in viluppi di seta
in arcobaleni di nastri risuonanti per forza di colore.
anche il caso bruciò, stoppino di candela, inquieto
nelle sue ombre, dalla polvere muove presenze
        infinite,
vuoto dopo vuoto costrette alla scala della materia.
tutto è pieno, lo sai, dal plancton al vassoio
che in un taglio di luce porta la testa del santo.
il magma si gonfia contro di noi, troppo hai cercato,
fra una meteora e l'altra, di darti una ragione, amore.
sogno lucente, forma, quiete, senso, il sentimento
ha interrotto, di misura in misura d'una nostra vita,
eruzioni e implosioni: sorridimi almeno, culmine
della natura, prima che tutto di noi torni materia inerte.

4.

cavallo marrone, imprigionato da pochi stecchi
dentro la dolina. chiusa la stretta via, trotti rotondo,
l'orizzonte di rocce scavate ruota con te, occhi
        d'ansia,
enormi di màcina, enormi di cavezza. sei solo, libero
come il calcare che si scioglie d'acqua, nel mezzo
un cranio di bue calcinato in eterno la sua ragione
        stilla.

FABIO DOPLICHER

in the glow of an oil-lamp, in tangles of silk
in rainbows of ribbons resounding by dint of color.
chance also burned, candle-wick restless
in its shadows, stirring from the dust infinite presences
forced onto the stairway of matter, void after void.
all is full, you know, from plankton to the platter
that in a ray of light bears the head of the saint.
the magma swells against us, you've tried too hard,
between one meteor and the next, to find a reason, love.
shining dream, form, peace, sense, sentiment
has ceased the eruptions and implosions, from measure to
    measure
of this our life: smile at me, at least, O summit
of nature, before all in us returns to inert matter.

4.

chestnut horse, imprisoned by a few sticks
in the sink-hole. the narrow path closed off, you trot roundly,
the horizon of unearthed rocks turns round with you, eyes of
    distress
gaping wide with the burden, wide with the halter. you're
    alone, free
as the limestone that dissolves with water. midway

cenere del pensiero, ignea scintilli e poi ricadi
compatta ti scolpisci in un granello. una solitaria
nuca di guerra, cotta dal sole, uguale a tante altre,
il giustiziato chissà perché, fra tutti i mattoni abband
     onati,
all'imbocco del viottolo di roccia. il muratore adesso
è poltiglia, inquieta molla della materia. genera radici
a forma d'uomo, intatte dalla terra le strappa un bimbo,
laggiù, girando come un cavallo, compatto nel suo
     orizzonte.
squarcio dopo squarcio, incolliamo lembi di pelle
con puntine di ferro rugginose, quelle lontane, fra le nebbie
del porto in scatoline strane sparpagliate, sospese col sogno.

(1980)

FABIO DOPLICHER

an ox-skull calcined for eternity distills its reason.
ash of thought, you sparkle igneous and then fall again,
sculpting yourself compact in a grain. a solitary
nape of war, baked by the sun like so many others,
a man put to death, who knows why, among all the
    abandoned bricks
at the entrance to the lane of stones. the mason now
is mush, matter's restless mainspring. he grows man-shaped
roots, a child pulls them up whole from the earth,
over there, running about like a horse, compact in his horizon.
gash after gash, we pin up strips of skin
with rusty thumb-tacks, distant ones, amid the harbor's
mists in strange little boxes strewn about and suspended by
    dream.

(Stephen Sartarelli)

FABIO DOPLICHER

A S I M M E T R I A   D E L L ' U N I V E R S O

Dopo un millesimo di secondo
il mondo era già determinato.
Nello squilibrio della materia, il vuoto
nasceva dentro l'ignoto portatore di leggi.
Contenitore del tempo consumato, ho amato
la necessità del verso, specchio dell'energia.
Non sei solo parola, parola mia.

Oggi chi giace con te, poesia,
è uno strano equilibrista del desiderio.
M'impongo di esser serio, perché nel gelido spazio
la luce incorrotta mi raggiunga con la lunga parabola.
Siamo lo specchio inutile e necessario,
candidati all'ossario dopo le alchimie del canto.
Ma, intanto, cerca l'orlo del pensabile e vola.

Attorcigliando una ciocca fra l'anulare e il mignolo,
mi chiedi dove andiamo. Siamo come i versi,
liberati e persi in questi secchi colmi d'acqua.
Non vorrei rispecchiarmi, la rosura di un giorno
non colma l'arsura dentro di noi, fattasi quiete.
Felicità di pensare, priva di mète,
musica lontana da noi, anticristalli.

FABIO DOPLICHER

ASYMMETRY OF THE UNIVERSE

In a thousandth of a second
the world was already made.
in matter's imbalance, the void
was born within the unknown lawgiver.
Vessel of time spent, I've loved
the necessity of verse, mirror of energy.
You're not just word, my word.

Today he who lies with you, poetry,
walks an odd tightrope of desire.
It's seriousness I require, so that in the icy space
untainted light may reach me with its long parabola.
We are the useless, necessary mirror,
ossuary-bound after alchemies of song.
But seek for now the boundary of the thinkable and soar.

Twisting a curl between ring-finger and pinky,
you ask me where we're going. We're like verses,
free, dispersed in buckets abrim with water.
I don't want to see my reflection, a day's gnawing
does not satisfy our clawing thirst, now grown calm.
Happiness of thinking without goal, balm
of music far away, anticrystals.

FABIO DOPLICHER

Un ladro in guanti gialli, ecco il poeta, costretto,
negli alberghi della cité bergère, ai rituali
ai calendari agli oneri sociali ai formulari
burocratici. Una diversa creazione, urla
l'immaginazione e si masturba,
contestatrice invecchiata, invano
incatenata da due assessori.

Come nel passaggio da un piano all'altro
il raggio si scompone, adesso la poesia
cerca brevissimi intervalli. La pulsazione
ha periodi netti, i costruttori di versi
orientano i propri radar nello stagno quotidiano.
Nel pantano, non c'è scelta: essere Dio
oppure un cacciatore di rane.

Il senso della fine domina
tutti i nostri sensi. Nomina parole,
si cela fra pensiero e corpo, li scuote
entrambi. A tasche vuote, i chierichetti
dell'ineffabile spifferano soletti fra i muri
del convento. Un altro vento, cosmico,
lontano, rende vano e risibile ogni affanno.

A ciascuno il suo danno, Orfeo sulla bilancia
pesa la disponibilità a sopravviversi
dei falsi loici e dei finti iniziati:

FABIO DOPLICHER

A thief in yellow gloves, that's the poet, in the hotels
of the cité bergère, forced into the rituals, the programes,
the social duties, the bureaucratic
forms. A different creation, shouts
the imagination, masturbating,
aged radical, as in vain
two councilmen apply the chains.

As in the passage from one plane to another
a beam of light is broken, so poetry now seeks
the briefest intervals. The pulsation
has distant cycles; verse-builders
orient their radar in the bog of the ordinary.
In marshland, there's no choice: one must be
God or a frog-hunter.

A sense of the end reigns over
all our senses. It names words,
hides between thought and body, rocks
them both. With empty pockets, altar boys
of the ineffable whisper all in solitude
within the monastery walls. Another wind, cosmic
and distant, makes trepidation useless and laughable.

To each his own downfall, Orpheus on the scales
weighs the chances of the false logicians
and the sham initiates to survive one another:

se preparati non siete a morire
non tentate il canto. Il manto
sfilacciato dell'ozono ci espone
senza scampo a un mutato ciclo.

Arte del pensiero che t'affatichi
dentro questa età mezzana. Al culmine
della frana, la materia risucchia e più non vedi.
Cedi a poco a poco, ricominci il gioco:
ha un respiro di mare questo venire e cercare.
Dentro la cornice della pagina
il verso impigrisce e sogna.

Dispersi nel gelo, dove più larghe
le maglie della materia irradiano,
i nostri pensieri captano solitudine.
Non c'è corrispondenza neppure all'origine,
e noi, giocatori incattiviti,
puntiamo tutta la posta sull'equilibrio.
Ma il canto vero costa una divina disarmonia.

Il bianco non esiste, eppure, creature della pagina
cerchiamo oltre i margini. I dintorni della poesia,
visitatrice occulta, sacra prostituta.
Se non t'aiuta quella passione
non cercar canzone o pianto.
L'incanto di due innamorati,
compagna mia, sta oltre l'amplesso.

FABIO DOPLICHER

if you're not prepared to die
do not attempt the song. The ozone's
ragged veil leaves us inescapably exposed
to an alteration in the cycle.

Art of thought you toil hard
inside this intermediary age. At the peak
of landslide, matter engulfs and you see no more.
Slowly you subside, begin the game again:
there's a breath of sea in this repeated seeking.
Within the page's frame the verses
idle and begin to dream.

Scattered in ice, where the links
of matter's chain radiate more broadly,
our thoughts tune into solitude.
There is no correspondence, not even with the source,
and we, the embittered gamblers,
we bet all our chips on balance
though true song needs divine disharmony.

White does not exist and yet, creatures of the page,
we search beyond the margins—the outskirts of poetry,
occult visitress, sacred prostitute.
If that passion is of no help to you
seek no song or complaint.
The spell of two persons in love,
my friend, lies beyond the coupling.

FABIO DOPLICHER

Dentro la sua matrice rifluisce la materia vecchia,
si condensa. L'intensa attrazione della meta
tutto riduce a questo estremo spazio.
Sazio di corpi, gelido, s'avvicina
il dèmone del pensiero. Offre
un nero margine d'incompiutezza:
ma la libertà non attira, manca la forma.

Come in una notte serena
il cielo indica i varchi dell'immaginazione
e la simulazione del vuoto a quella rete
ci riconduce, adesso la ragione della poesia
diventa contemplazione amorosa
del margine dei disperati, dei versi pensati,
degli anni persi in un anello.

Alchimisti del bello senza pietra di paragone,
diamoci la mano, ragazza, davanti al notturno
Canopo d'Adriano. Non conta rifare,
dalla vasca di mercurio occorre
sollevare un nuovo omuncolo.
Così sulla via proveremo la parola,
dandoci la mano verso la torre di Chia.

(1984)

FABIO DOPLICHER

Into its matrix the old matter flows back,
condenses. The goal's intense attraction
leads everything back to this outermost space.
Sated with bodies, ice-cold, the demon
of thought draws near. He offers
a black margin of incompleteness;
but freedom does not attract: form is missing.

As when on a clear night
the sky reveals the imagination's openings
and the simulation of the void takes us back
to that net, so poetry's concern has now
become the loving contemplation
of the margins of the hopeless, of verses
thought, years wasted in a ring.

Alchemists of beauty with no touchstone,
let us join hands, my girl, before Hadrian's
nocturnal Canopus. Imitation doesn't count:
from the pool of mercury we must
raise up a new homunculus.
And so along the way shall we test the word
as we join hands toward the tower of Chia.

(Stephen Sartarelli)

DISSONANZE

Hai piantato la vita, zolla
protetta in una rete di paglia.
Guardavi quel tronco esile
senza foglie né gemme:
cieco, non provava vergogna.

La vite americana si propaga,
infetta i mattoni di verde,
d'inverno su àgoli di foglie
rinsecchita dorme: il suo io
verde sprofondato in fioriere
di cemento, col taglio netto
della via delle formiche.

L'umana pianta penetra armadi,
i doppifondi dei topi, dei matti.
Chiusi nelle scatole-stanze, soli,
controllati dal televisore
sempre baluginante. Un petalo
verde-pastello si apre, posa
sulla palma di un matto in età.

La legge degli aghi di pino,
un tenero equilibrio sul balcone,
a ogni ventata ritrova l'ordine.

DISCORDS

You planted life, protecting
its soil with a net of straw.
You watched that slender trunk
without leaves or buds:
blind, it felt no shame.

The American vine spreads out,
infecting the bricks with green,
dry in the winter it sleeps
under needle-like leaves: its green
self submerged in concrete
flowerpots, neatly crossed
by the pathways of ants.

The human plant penetrates wardrobes,
double-bottomed cages of mice, of madmen.
Closed in box-like rooms, alone,
watched by perpetually blinking
televisions. A pastel-green
petal opens itself, resting
on the palm of an aged madman.

The law of the pine needles,
the balcony's fragile equilibrium,
with every gust restores its order.

Nulla è solo in quei ramoscelli,
la resina goccia, ferite natalizie.
Il silenzio si infila nel silenzio.
Il silenzio pettina il silenzio.

Sul tetto le talee spingono radici
nel rivestimento d'amianto:
altri individui, piante di vita
mutàgene sotto l'antenna radio,
che la notte accende in conversari.
La voce è una forma, aquila
irriconoscibile dai nemici di terra.

Sul verdissimo puntale l'arancio
invelenisce fiore dopo fiore,
rinselva, a mezza simulazione
di natura. Dentro l'artificio
di pietra e di ferro, sbaglia
per amore. Pure aspro, urticato
dai vetri, ha morbidi vagiti.

La scorza in sottili filigrane,
fruttifica un solo àcino,
si guarda col solitario occhio,
da lui si stacca. La osserva,

FABIO DOPLICHER

Nothing is alone in those twigs,
the resin drips like birth wounds.
The silence threads itself through silence.
The silence combs the silence.

On the roof the cuttings thrust
their roots into the asbestos insulation:
other individuals, mutated,
plants of life beneath the radio antenna
which the night ignites into colloquy.
The voice is a form, an eagle
unrecognized by the enemies of earth.

On its greenest branch-top the orange tree
becomes embittered with flower after flower,
growing leaves again, a half simulation
of nature. Inside the artifice
of stone and iron it makes mistakes
for love. Though harsh, venomed
by glass, it has soft whimpers.

The bark in subtle filigree
produces a single grape,
watches itself with a solitary eye,
it breaks off. It watches her

FABIO DOPLICHER

a galla nella grondaia, nei fili
di sequenze, per un lunghissimo
istante. Tanta corteccia, grumi,
nòduli, semenza. Il cuore è nodo:
quante cannucce, palude d'aria.

(1988)

FABIO DOPLICHER

float in the gutter, in threads
of sequence, for the longest
of instants. Such bark, clots,
knots, seed. The heart is a knot:
so many reeds, swamps of air.

(Dana Gioia)

NOTES ON THE POEMS

From "Unfinished Exile"

La Risiera refers to La Risiera di San Sbba, a Nazi concentration camp in the Friuli region of northern Italy.

From "Asymmetry of the Universe"

Among the theories of contemporary physics concerning the origin of the universe, there is one [explored by Andrej Sakharov, among others] which situates it in an *asymmetry* in the corresponding quantities of matter and antimatter at an instant one thousandth of a second after the initial "big bang." [Author's note]

The emperor Hadrian gave the name of *Canopus* to a part of his villa in Tivoli, where numerous Egyptian antiques were collected; *Canopus* was an ancient city of the western Egyptian delta. *Canopus* is also a bright star in the Argo constellation, situated in the rudder of the ship.

Chia is a town in northern Latium, near Viterbo. [Translator's note]

UMBERTO PIERSANTI

UMBERTO PIERSANTI

CRITICAL NOTE

Umberto Piersanti teaches the sociology of literature and art at the University of Urbino, the city where he was born in 1941. Precocious and prolific, he published *All'ora del crepuscolo* (In the Hour of Twilight), the first of his eight collections of poetry, at the age of twenty-five. Recognition came slowly at first, since the traditional qualities of his poetry put him at odds with what he described as "the obsessive experimentalism of the neo-avantgarde." Ironically, he has also been criticized by the opposite camp for what some see as too casual a handling of traditional metrics. But Piersanti's work gradually established itself in contemporary letters. His poetry is now represented in anthologies both in Italy and throughout Europe. His work has been the subject of critical articles and of a monograph in the *Oltre il Novecento* series of studies of contemporary poets, and several of his recent volumes have won prestigious awards. He has also published two books of essays and edited, with Fabio Doplicher, an anthology of contemporary Italian poetry. He is the author of the film *L'eta breve*, produced in 1969, and of several "film-poems" (his term for a short film in which a poetic atmosphere takes precedence over plot) which have been broadcast in the last several years. Three of his other screenplays appeared in 1985 in the anthology *Cinema e poesia negli anni 1980*.

As might be expected from his interest in art and film, Piersanti's poetry is richly descriptive, deeply rooted in the senses and the physicality of nature. Piersanti is also self-consciously a regional poet. His writing celebrates the particular beauties of his native city of Urbino, his "point of departure and return for excursions in the great world," and the Renaissance landscape of Montefeltro. Though charged at times with an intense sexuality, his work often recalls the poetry of seventy-five or even one hundred years ago. From the title of his first collection to the imagery of some of his latest and finest poems, one might draw a connection between Piersanti and the so-called "Crepuscular School" of Guido Gozzano (Italy's great turn-of-the-century poet whose work resembles that of Jules Laforgue and the early T.S. Eliot). Common to both poets is the leisurely, often poignant exploration of the landscapes of memory, lit in twilight tones, and colored with autumnal shades. In renewing this tradition, Piersanti draws on the powers of the past to give expression to timeless human longings. He is an uncharacteristic contemporary poet, but out of his determined individuality comes his artistic authenticity.

—M.P.

POETRY

All'ora del crepuscolo. Urbino, 1966.

La breve stagione. Urbino, 1967.

Il tempo differente. Caltanissetta-Rome, 1974.

L'urlo della mente. Florence, 1977.

Nascere nel '40. Milan, 1981.

Natura morta con paesaggio. Urbino, 1983.

Passaggio di sequenza. Bologna, 1986.

Per tempi e luoghi. Bergamo, 1988.

OTHER

L'ambigua presenza (essays). Rome, 1980.

Sul limite d'ombra (essays). Bologna, 1989.

QUANDO L'OTTOBRE
LENTO TRASCOLORA

è come il mosto dolce che le vespe
coprono fitte e ingorde dentro il fumo
tenue d'ottobre ch'entra nelle stalle
il sole ch'ha oscurato qui la bacca
del biancospino è viola ormai la polpa
là sopra il cono d'erbe dove cessa
questo delle Cesane il più bel monte
sotto lo spino bianco il seno nudo
gode gli odori tiepidi nell'aria
caldo è il mio bianco sangue fra gli umori

scesi con il crepuscolo tra i rovi
fummo dentro un sentiero colmo d'erbe
e la cicoria ancora s'alza azzurra
dentro la guazza nel mese non suo
l'ombra era scesa lunga sul maggese
alto ormai nella notte e rilevato
vede la Grazia il segno e gli gravava
sempre fino dagli anni in cui soleva
stringere dentro il nastro i suoi capelli
feci cenno col capo solo ho detto
ch'ho sentito talora tra le volte
verso quest'ora un suono dolce e chiaro

UMBERTO PIERSANTI

WHEN SLOW OCTOBER CHANGES COLOR

It's like the sweet must that wasps
cover thick and greedy in the soft October
mist as it drifts into the stables
the sun that here has darkened
the hawthorn berry's pulp is now violet
over the cone of grasslands where ends
this most beautiful of the Cesana mountains
under the white thorn the naked breast
enjoys the tepid odors in the air
my white blood is warm among the humors

Fallen with the dusk amid the brambles
we were on a footpath brimming with grass
where the chicory still grows blue
in heavy dew in a month not its own
shadows had fallen long across the fallow ground
rising high in the night and upturned
Grace sees the sign that has burdened her
ever since the years when she used to
tie her hair up in a ribbon
I nodded my head and only said
that at times around this hour I heard
a sound sweet and clear among the vaults

UMBERTO PIERSANTI

bastonavamo il noce ch'era notte
e mentre cade s'apre il mallo scuro
dice non lo recorda — certo mai le lunghe
mani ha intriso nel suo verde—
e scosciavano i colpi dentro l'erbe
si perdevano i gusci nello scuro
solo il tuo riso scese fino ai greppi

un po' più tardi in mezzo alla radura
dentro il sentiero d'erbe che ci passa
s'accesero i cespugli con i canti
prima un trillo leggero che poi scroscia
e per la macchia fitta si risponde

le ciliegie di mare ancora gialle
ottobre le ha striate di vario rosso
scendono dal corbezzolo coi gambi
lunghi che il vento muove sopra l'onde
una che l'ho sospesa alle tue labbra
e ci baciamo dentro la sua polpa

ero tornato con mia madre dove
si torce la vitalba fin sui rovi
questa macchia è la mia qui ho ricercato

UMBERTO PIERSANTI

we used to thrash the walnut tree at night
the dark hulls opening as they fall
she says she doesn't remember—certainly
she's never dipped her long hands in its green—
the blows thundered in the grass
shells were lost in the darkness
and only your smile went down to the banks

a bit later in the middle of the glade
along the grassy path running through it
the bushes lit up with a singing
first a faint trill then a thunder
bursting through the thicket in reply

October has striped in motley red
the still yellow arbutus berries
from the strawberry tree they fall with long stems
that the wind moves over the billows
I've hung one from your lips
and we kiss in its pulp

I had returned with my mother to the place
where virgin's-bower even twists about the brambles
this thicket is my own and here I've looked

il fungo ch'è tra i carpini sottile
quando con la mia nonna ci s'alzava
verso le quattro l'erba che fumava
ma lei più nulla scorge dalla casa
scialbata e bianca dove è andata a stare
non gli sfuggiva una noce dentro l'erbe
e non perdeva un nido tra le canne
superati da tempo i novant'anni
quasi tutta la vista gli si è spenta

con le feste dei morti a fine ottobre
più volte allora scesi nella Torre
scorre sul vetro chiara la Cesana
lo scotano che segna il nostro autunno
dentro tutte le macchie oltre i lubàchi
dalle querce trapela rosso acceso
per la mia casa persa oltre la costa
da dove scendi parte uno stradino
lungo che giù precipita col fosso
ora nell'aria il sorbo odora quasi
come i suoi frutti dentro la mia stanza

scende quieta la luce alle Cesane
solo da qualche parte il cielo è acceso

UMBERTO PIERSANTI

for mushrooms that stand thin among the hornbeams
when with grandmother we used to get up
at four to mist-covered grasslands
but she sees nothing any more from the whitewashed
house where she has gone to stay
she never used to miss a single walnut
in the grass or nest among the reeds
she's well past ninety now
and almost all her vision's gone

at Halloween in late October
I often went down to the Tower
the Cesana ridge runs clear on the glass
the smoke-tree announcing our autumn
in all the thickets beyond the wind-furrows
oozes bright red among the oaks
past my house lost beyond the slope
a long narrow road on the way down the hill
plunges deep with the gully below
in the air the sorb now smells almost
like its fruits inside my room

light falls softly on the mountains
only here and there is the sky still bright

s'alza a quest'ora sempre un po' di bruma
quando l'ottobre lento trascolora
nei fumi grigio scuri di novembre
Urbino nella conca ha pochi lumi
passa dentro la notte e il temporale
ch'oltre quei monti lontano s'addensa
è questo tempo oscuro che lo cerchia
e dagli spazi vari ci minaccia
resta solo il profilo della grazia
l'acqua del fosso che più fresca odora

(metà ottobre 1983)

UMBERTO PIERSANTI

at this hour a bit of fog always rises
when slow October changes color
and becomes November's dark grey mists
Urbino in the valley has few lights
it passes into night and the storm
gathering afar beyond these hills
it's this somber weather all around it
that threatens us from the various spaces
a profile of grace is all that remains
the water of the gully smelling fresher

(Stephen Sartarelli)

SECONDO PASSAGGIO DI SEQUENZA

Murge che hai bianchi i sassi e verdi olivi
il tardo autunno solo conoscevi
dal cielo ch'era carico di grigi
e dalla vite rossa che splendeva
lungo i tuoi dossi d'erba scarsa e accesa
verso Castel del Monte la ghiandaia scende
bianca la coda fin dentro i pini
pungeva l'aria nera nello spiazzo

per le tue stanze immense giravamo
nella gran volta un'aria che filtrava
dentro i muri possenti tra la pietra
presso la feritoia t'ho scoperte
bianche le cosce lunghe e intiepidite
e t'ho goduta subito guardavo
oltre i capelli un pino nel dirupo

in questi stessi giorni nelle coste
che tutt'attorno scendono ai miei fossi
banchi di passeri volano sui raspi
ultimi nelle viti e i fichi marci
cresce la nebbia fitta ogni mattina
sale da sopra l'acque ma non copre

UMBERTO PIERSANTI

SECOND IMAGE SEQUENCE

Murge with your white stones and green olives
you knew only late autumn
from a sky laden with greys
and from the red grapevine that shone
across your hills of spare, bright grass
toward Castel del Monte the jay descends
white tail down among the pines
the black air bristled in the clearing

through your vast rooms we wandered
in the great vault of air that seeped
inside the powerful walls amid the stone
near the loophole I uncovered white
your long and tepid thighs
and savored you at once I saw
beyond your hair a pine tree in the crag

these same days on the hillsides
that everywhere slope down to my ditches
flocks of sparrows hover over grape-stalks
the last to reach the vines and rotten figs
the fog grows thick each morning
it rises from above the waters but doesn't cover

la grande macchia dove stanno i sorbi
il suo frutto caduto manda odore
azzurro d'aria intrisa nella terra
la verga d'oro ch'è l'ultimo fiore
sparge per tutti i campi i cespi spenti

scende precoce autunno sulle Ardenne
sparge di foglie gialle i corti laghi
s'alza in quei giorni rosso l'epilobio
accende il cuore fresco di settembre
nelle azzurre radure fra le querce
torno lungo i tuoi viali Mosa quieta
dolce s'appanna la città di sera
riempie chioschi e portoni di ragazze
bevono bionda birra contro i vetri
dov'è accennata l'acqua per le luci

per un portone liberty s'entrava
nella tua stanza sempre un poco scura
il crepuscolo scende già alle cinque
nello spiazzo deserto sopra il muro
dove s'accenna a un bosco che si perde
Gaetan in quei giorni io te e Lucia
siamo saliti per le vie e gli orti
che il primo autunno striscia dei suoi rossi

UMBERTO PIERSANTI

the great thicket where the sorbs stand
their fallen fruit casting an azure
odor of air sodden in earth
the goldenrod, the final flower
strews its spent tufts over the fields

autumn descends early on the Ardennes
strews the brief lakes with yellow leaves
the willow-herb rises red around that time
lights up September's cool heart
in the azure glades amid the oaks
I'm back along your avenues, gentle Meuse
the city softly mists over in evening
filling kiosks and doorways with young girls
they drink golden beer against the windows
in which the water is hinted by the lights

through a nouveau doorway one entered
your always slightly shadowed room
twilight's already fallen by five
in the deserted space above the wall
that suggests a wood disappearing in the distance
around that time you, Gaetan, Lucia and I
went up the streets and past the orchards
striped by early autumn's reds

s'alzavano le cupole di Liegi
dai basamenti scuri oltre quel velo
lieve di nebbia o fumo che si spande

quella città del nord ha i cieli chiari
che di pioggia improvvisa il vento oscura
dalle sue acque escono i palazzi
che il platano nei viali ammorbidisce
c'era un airone fermo sul gradino
oltre l'ultima casa l'oceano nero

passa il maschio meschino a gruppi stenti
lungo i canali sporchi come il riso
creatura superba che ti dai
per quattro soldi e fissi noi dal vetro
pieghi il tuo corpo forte ai ciechi gridi
spenti dopo l'amplesso ci sovrasti

l'ultimo ciclo chiude quando torna
novembre oggi che splende come mai
brilla la quercia nella foglia secca
dentro l'azzurro limpido che sale
e sotto i peri accesi il crisantemo
bianco si spande e giallo dentro l'erba
oggi i miei colli viola oltre i colori

UMBERTO PIERSANTI

the domes of Liège rose up
from their dark basements
beyond the spreading veil of fog or smoke

that Northern city has clear skies
which the wind darkens with sudden rain
from its waters emerge buildings
softened by the plane trees on the avenues
a heron stood motionless on the stair
beyond the last house the black ocean

wretched males pass by in awkward groups
along canals dirty as laughter
proud creature, you give yourself
for two bits and stare at us through glass
bending your strong body to the blind shouts
fading after coupling you rise above us

the final cycle ends today
with November's return more radiant than ever
the oak glistens in the withered leaf
within the limpid blue sky rising
and under vivid pear trees the chrysanthemum
spreads white and yellow in the grass
today my hills a violet beyond all color

m'hanno gonfiato il cuore avrei voluto
la mia vicenda eterna e le figure
col loro corpo scendere di nuovo
per tutti i greppi e i prati degli amori
il gelo che oltre i monti già ci aspetta
brucerà il verde rigide le piante
voglio fissarti vita nella luce
voglio fermarti prima della sera

(1984)

UMBERTO PIERSANTI

have weighed upon my heart I wished
my story to be eternal and the figures
to descend with their bodies again
over all the slopes and meadows of loves
the frost in store for us beyond the mountains
will burn the green plants stiff
I want to gaze upon you in the light, life
I want to stop you before evening

(Stephen Sartarelli)

UMBERTO PIERSANTI

PER TEMPI E LUOGHI

c'era la palma sola o a branchi radi
ma so che oltre quel cerchio essa non cresce
resta la sabbia nuda, la distesa
dove affondi la gamba, dov'è scesa
la donna corsa avanti che s'arresta
sgomenta nell'Aperto che la cerchia

il suono monocorde dell'azzurro
che s'alza nel silenzio fino al cielo
senza una striscia bianca, senza una piuma
è come questa febbre che m'appanna
poeta che conosci il deserto vasto
ci sono stato io una volta sola
come turista che si serra ai vetri
nel lungo viaggio dove è il più solo
trasale per la febbre e lo sgomento
c'era prima un villaggio calcinato
come talvolta vedi nei presepi
ma qui non scorre l'acqua, non c'è il mulino
trapassa nell'azzurro anche la terra
verde no, ma rossiccia come capra
e la viola africana gigantesca
anche lei nell'azzurro ci si staglia

IN TIMES AND PLACES

There was the solitary palm, or scattered clumps
yet I know they don't grow outside that circle
there's only naked sand there, a broad expanse
that swallows your step, where running ahead
a woman descends and comes to a stop,
frightened by the open space surrounding her

the blue sky's monotonal hum
rising up in silence to the heavens
without a shred of white or single feather
is like the fever misting over me
poet versed in the desert and its vastness
I myself was there only once
as a tourist self-enclosed in glass
on a long journey where he's the most alone
twitching with fever and consternation
first there was a chalk-white little village
of the sort you sometimes see in creches
but no water flows here, there's no water-mill
even the earth not green but pale red
like she-goats transpierces the sky's blue
and even the giant African violets
stand out distinct against the blue

è stato un lungo viaggio prima gli olivi
poi una landa con il vento freddo
e le piane di sale bianche e perfette
la febbre la portò quell'aria ghiaccia
spira lungo il gran disco che m'abbaglia
per il suo cupo caldo e la sua luce

un solo dio abita il deserto
e compone i miraggi, alza la sabbia
entra dentro la tenda pervade il sogno
del pastore di popoli e di greggi
dio dell'imperio sa che nel deserto
vince la sabbia e vince nel pianeta

ma nei miei boschi passano gli dei
stanno dentro le fonti e nelle grotte
s'accostano improvvisi nel cammino
di rado sono saggi, pronti al riso
all'ira e all'amplesso cogli umani

Cerveteri ricordo, cogli asfodeli su tumuli
rotondi, l'erba che scende, il solco di quel carro
che si perde nelle strade dei morti incontro ai vivi
e io passo con te mia bionda amica tra le rose canine,

UMBERTO PIERSANTI

it was a long trip, first the olive trees
then a heathland blowing with a cold wind
and the salt-flats gleaming white and perfect
that icy air brought on the fever
gusting beside the great disk that dazzled
with its gloomy warmth and strange light

one god alone inhabits the desert
and fashions mirages, raises the sand
that enters the tent and pervades the dreams
of the shepherd of peoples and flocks
the god of the empire knows that in the desert
the sand always wins, shall win the planet

but in my woodlands the gods move about,
hiding in grottoes and wellsprings in earth
they appear of a sudden on the footpaths
seldom wise, ever quick to laughter
and to anger and coupling with humans

I remember Cerveteri and the asphodels on round
tumuli, the grass sloping down and the ruts of a cart
vanishing into streets of the dead toward the living
while I move with you my blonde amid the dog-roses,

tra fiori bianchi e quel cespuglio d'acanto
che chiude la nostra storia alle voci d'intorno

conobbero il deserto anche gli etruschi
o com'era il deserto quando d'intorno
scorrevano i ruscelli e nel palmeto
la timida cerbiatta s'addentrava
prima che arrivasse quel solo dio
che non ama l'idillio ma che parla
dai rovi o tra la sabbia o la tempesta

dentro l'ultima tenda l'etrusco vede
l'anatra colorata appesa al palo
fitti di voli i cieli di Maremma
colmi di pesci tutti i rivi chiari
porta nella sua tomba la cara vita
l'avrà fissa d'intorno per l'eterno

ad Achille pensavo, alla grande ombra mesta
nei Campi Elisi, e mi cerchiava l'erba luminosa
maggio di tutti i mesi il più gonfio e verde
meglio fare il porcaro nel caldo sole
che principe dei morti per l'Ade grigio
caddero i giovinetti nello Scamandro
e fu l'ultimo fiato di rimpianto

UMBERTO PIERSANTI

through white flowers and an acanthus bush
that closes our story to the voices around us

the Etruscans as well knew the desert
or what the desert was like when streams flowed
all round it and the timid young doe
lightly entered the palm-grove
a few steps ahead of that lone god
who cares little for idylls but speaks
from brambles or through the sand or the storm

inside the last tent the Etruscan sees
a colorful duck hung from a pole
the skies of Maremma teeming with flight
the clear brooks all brimming with fish
he takes dear life down with him into his grave
he'll have it thereafter forever around him

I was thinking of Achilles, of that great mournful shade
in the Elysian Fields, with the bright grass around me
May the greenest, most swollen month of all
better to be a swineherd in the hot sun
than prince of the dead for gloomy Hades
when the young boys fell into the Scamander
regret gave out its final breath

in un lontano autunno ero venuto
qui con Rosaria, il tempo differente
era morto per sempre ma da poco
per il nero sgomento che mi colse
io guardavo il tuo corpo grande e scuro
lo specchio che era dietro, il mare in fondo
quel tuo corpo in cui entro e mi ci stringo
il solo che mi stacchi dalla catena
i tuoi capelli sono come arbusti
che io afferro e tormento e poi odoro

ho rivisto poi la chiesa quadra
s'alza potente e chiara sulle mura
ha in faccia il mare etrusco verderame
un ceppo di giusquiamo era filtrato
dalla sua pietra bianca gode la luce

il tondo lago di Bracciano è specchio
alle selve d'intorno, tra i grandi ontani
solo un momento ti saresti distesa
per un istante solo t'avrei colta
così assoluta e tesa nel lucore
che trapassa le erbe, mescola il giallo
della prima ginestra al miele della pelle
ai capelli biondissimi che sanno di ramo nuovo
        e foglia

one autumn long ago I came here
with Rosaria, different time was dead
forever but hadn't been so for long
from the black dismay that overcame me
I gazed at your body, so large and dark,
and at the mirror behind, and the distant sea
that body I enter inside and cling to
the only one that can ever unchain me
your hair is like a thicket of shrubs
that I grab and twist and then inhale

later I saw the quadrangular church
rising bright and potent upon the walls
before it lies the verdigris Etruscan sea
a stump of black henbane had filtered through
the white stone and basked in the sunlight

the round lake of Bracciano is a mirror
to the woods around it, among the great alders
you would lie down only for a moment
and only for an instant would I pluck you there
so tense and absolute in the shimmer
radiating from the grasses, blending
the early broom's yellow with the honey of your skin
and blond hair that smelled of young branches
        and leaves

UMBERTO PIERSANTI

quindi un quieto paese in fondo al lago
come altre volte mi stringeva il cuore
che ce ne andiamo e il cielo quasi piove

il tuo corpo e le erbe i campi e i fiori
tutto trascorre è tempo di tornare
parto questa volta di primavera
i prati sono gialli per le rape
ma come allora scorgo l'Appennino
che addensa nubi e nebbie alle sue cime

(1987)

UMBERTO PIERSANTI

and a peaceful town at the bottom of the lake
as at other times like this, my heart was aching
it's time for us to leave, the sky looks like rain

your body and the grasses, the fields and flowers
all passes on now it's time to go back
I am leaving in spring this time around
the meadows are yellow from the turnips
but as before I see again the Appenines
gathering clouds and mist around their summits

(Stephen Sartarelli)

UMBERTO PIERSANTI

NOTES ON THE POEMS

From "Second Image Sequence"

Murge: A region in the South of Italy.

Ardennes: A mountain range for the most part in Belgium, but which also runs into NE France and Luxemburg.

From "In Times and Places"

Scamander: The Scamander is the principal river of the Trojan plain.

Cerveteri: The site of a vast, well-preserved Etruscan necropolis.

LUIGI FONTANELLA

LUIGI FONTANELLA

CRITICAL NOTE

Luigi Fontanella was born in San Severino, near Salerno, in 1943. After completing his education in Rome, he earned a Ph.D. in Romance languages and literature at Harvard University. He was subsequently a Fulbright Fellow at Princeton University. Since 1982 he has taught Italian language and literature at the State University of New York at Stony Brook (Long Island), where he also edits the international literary review *Gradiva*. In addition to six volumes of poetry, Fontanella has published a collection of short stories, a novel, and a critical study; he is presently at work on a book about Pier Paolo Pasolini. His play, *Don Giovanni a New York* (*Don Juan in New York*), was one of four variations on the Don Juan theme by contemporary Italian writers commissioned and performed in Rome in 1988. A New York production in translation was mounted in 1990. Fontanella has also translated a great deal of poetry into Italian, including selections from the French Surrealists and contemporary American authors. Translations of his own poetry have appeared in France, England, Spain, the United States, and the Soviet Union. He lives in Monte Porzio, near Rome, with Rosanna Liberatore and their three-year-old daughter Emma.

The variety and breadth of Fontanella's literary activity are reflected in the context of his poetry, which ranges from complex sequences to epigrammatic "fragments," from hard-edged observations to tender expressions of family love (sometimes in the same poem). Though obviously modernistic in appearance and tendency, his work is nonetheless strongly, and at times subtly, grounded in traditional techniques. Fontanella often uses closing rhymes, especially in the more personal poems, and one hears a richness of assonance and internal rhyme. There is also a hendecasyllabic backbone to even the freest of his verses, and an occasional echo of classic forms, as in the *settenari* of "Turning of the car." Fontanella's openness to all possibilities also characterizes his literary criticism. While many critics promote a single aesthetic, he approves of the diversity of contemporary Italian poetry, finding all of the many different styles and modes potentially valid. Despite the time Fontanella has spent in the United States and the American references in some of his work, he dismisses all attempts to hyphenate him as a man of letters, observing that "no one ever classified Pound as anything but an American."

—M.P.

POETRY
La verifica incerta. Rome, 1972.
La vita trasparente. Venice, 1978.
Simulazione di reato. Manduria, 1979.
Fabula. Rome, 1980.
Stella Saturnina. Rome, 1989.
Round Trip. Udine, 1990.

OTHER
Il surrealismo italiano (criticism). Rome, 1983.
Milestone e altre storie. Siena-Rome, 1983.
Hot-Dog (novel). Rome, 1986.

LUIGI FONTANELLA

LA VITA TRASPARENTE

Apre la città le sue strade,
corrono biciclette senza persone,
alla finestra s'affaccia
e sparisce un volto di donna,
le vetrine offrono sessi
per ogni stagione,
giro di vite:
balla una coppia agile e magra
nella piazza deserta,
la corsa degli uomini,
agita chiome il bosco
in controluce,
passi su foglie
e solchi di fango duro,
viale d'autunno
carrozza regale
pioggia di rugiada
e di carta:
la vita trasparente.

(1977)

LUIGI FONTANELLA

THE   TRANSPARENT   LIFE

the city opens its streets,
bicycles go by riderless,
a woman's face in a window
appears then vanishes,
shop-windows offer fetishes
for every season,
lives turning,
a slender agile couple dances
in the deserted piazza,
the race men run,
the hairy woods shivering
against the grain of light,
footsteps on leaves
and furrows of stiff mud,
avenue of autumn
royal coach
rain of dew
and paper—
the transparent life.

(W.S. DiPiero)

SLEEPLESSNESS

1.

per ondate successive
quando a perdersi negli strati
basta uno scatto d'ansia
una sonnolenza insonne.
sul filo dei gradini
un velo di polvere attònita
e muta all'immagine improvvisa
l'ansare d'una corsa
rapida, sempre più,
lunga e distante
variegata nella brama
che gli anni non attenua.

2.

andamenti circolari circonfusi circoscritti
nel magma verbale ticchettìo
vibràfono a placche dove sempre
difficile appare la scelta tempestiva
la corsa senza traguardi, creativa
o narcisista la manìa dell'oltre
che sbranca sprezza che sfiacca

LUIGI FONTANELLA

SLEEPLESSNESS

1.

in subsequent waves
when a fit of anxiety is enough
to lose oneself
in the layers, a sleepless drowsiness,
on the tense outline of the steps
a veil of astonished dust,
and mute to the sudden sight
the panting of a speedy
every speedier race,
long and distant
variegated in the greed
that the years do not subdue.

2.

circular movements steeped in
the verbal magma-tapping
the keyed vibraphone where the
timely choice appears always difficult,
the race without a finish line, the
narcissistic mania of the beyond
that scatters scorn that slows

in un lumàre emergente
di còseparòle che tentano ogni volta
l'Es-proprio sintomo/morbo di Ganser.

3.

sempre più a capofitto
nell'incenerire alogico la sfumatura
che conta e trapianta altri
steli da crescere un giorno
un'ora interposta a fitte trame
d'infanzia calcolata: giri
perduti tra i cliché di fine d'anno
e senza uno sforzo apparente.

4.

per la strada annullata i soliti
percorsi mentali a moltiplicarsi
l'éderasfòglia in cataclismi
tollerati non in mano a criminali
travestiti s'offre il pulsare parlare del gelso
sottocasa: aspetta frutti
meccanici in dolci sapori di lunghe
ventate e inventa alfabeti
lo scoiattolo bruno
che s'annida annaspa s'avventa
su per le trame dei tronchi
        antenati

LUIGI FONTANELLA

in an emergent glow
wordthings that every time tempt
the expropriated Id symptom/syndrome of Ganser.

3.

more and more headlong
in the alogical incinerating, the nuance
that counts and transplants
other stems to grow one day
one hour interposed in thick plots
of calculated childhood: turnings
lost among the new year's
clichés and effortlessly apparent.

4.

on the blackened street the usual
mental processes multiply,
the ivyleaf in tolerated
cataclysms offers itself not
to the hands of disguised criminals,
the pulsating plaining of the mulberry
by the house waits for mechanical
fruits in sweet flavors of long
windgusts and invents alphabets,
the brown squirrel that
furrows flounders flings itself
on the net of the ancestral branches

LUIGI FONTANELLA

poi in vigile attesa al mio passo
che non indovina.

5.

oggi è festa, è festa, è festa:
la gente s'appresta s'affretta
(di poco) al giro cortese
che schianta ogni più fresca speranza.
occultarsi tra anni-tende
masturbando il tempo
che posa lunghedita raggianti
su pareti tappeti tavoli piante carte cartacce
pensieri.

6.

qui, nella blanda rete che incatena
giorni e speranze aggrovigliate
è breve l'àttimo-témpo
che vaporizza desideri e distanze:
un altro passaggio
poi un altro ancora
sul grandevetro dell'oggi
che fermo al disegno
col dito.
poi lo scivolare incontrollato.

(1977)

then in vigilant waiting for my step
that he doesn't decipher.

5.

today is a holiday, holiday, holiday
the people make ready make haste
(a bit) to the courtly spin
that crushes every fresher hope.
to hide among the year-curtains
masturbating time
that rests radiant fingerlengths
on the walls carpets tables plants letters papers
thoughts.

6.

here, in the mild net that enchains
days and tangled hopes
the split-second-time is brief
vaporizing desires
and distances: another passage
then another
on the picture window of the today
that I stop with a tracing
finger.
then the uncontrolled sliding.

(W.S. DiPiero)

DOPO LA FESTA

e dunque gli altri se ne andarono prima
le bocche aperte al sonno dei grilli
ed io qui a discernere steli
da rendere credibili alla luce,
quest'impossibilità di rovesciare
il corso dei tanti minuti gocciole
che s'ingrossano lungo le discese viziate,
a quanti poi il merito
dopo la caduta. Ma noi imperterriti qui,
la faccia ai muri
soffocando la bocca di lei che
dal letto o dal cesso chiama
e richiama. Ogni notte così.
E' un inganno quest'appuntamento
che si ripete agli occhi,
è lotta che smembra che spossa
sempre sul filo teso in un difficile
esercizio che apre ogni volta
una ferita o una speranza diversa:
è gioco, un duello,
un ritornello antico a cui non so rifiutarmi,
debolezze da romantico attardato
non guarirò mai da questo male.
Giro la sveglia, sta' calma, ancora

LUIGI FONTANELLA

AFTER THE PARTY

and so the others were the first to leave
their mouths opening toward cricket-sleep and I'm
still here separating a bunch of flower stems
to make each believable to the light,
this impossibility of turning back
the flooding minutes the droplets swelling
along the ruined paths of descent,
but what's it all worth
after the fall. And yet we're fearless here,
face to the wall
stifling her mouth when she calls
and calls from the bed
or bathroom. Every night like this.
It's a trick, this arrangement
flashing again and again before my eyes,
an exhausting fight, tearing things apart,
always on a taut wire performing
a difficult exercise that inevitably opens
a different wound or hope.
It's a game, a duel
an old refrain I can't resist,
romantic loitering and all its weakness,
I'll never be cured of this disease.
I set the alarm, take it easy, just

LUIGI FONTANELLA

un momento, poi ti raggiungo.
Non c'è da stare allegri:
avvengono cose che non si riconoscono
subito, di «primo acchito»,
chi l'avrebbe detto stamattina
il gatto morto stecchito,
a pancia all'aria, e tutto in una notte;
ho ancora il suo graffio sulla mano
che ieri scherzando (?) m'ha fatto,
lo guardo di nuovo questo graffio
quest'incrostatura sberleffo
questo piccolo Burri
sulla mia mano sinistra.
Vedi, basta poco, già ricomincio a viaggiare:
è già tanto se la poesia ti porta
a piacere, attimo e forza di vivere
un solo momento. E vieni a letto ch'è tardi.

(1978-1979)

LUIGI FONTANELLA

a minute and I'll get back to you.
Nothing to feel happy about—
thing happen that you don't recognize
right away or on the spot,
who would have said it this morning
the cat stone dead,
belly up, and all in one night:
I still have the scratch on my hand
that he gave me (joking?) yesterday,
I look again at the scratch,
this sneering incrustation,
this little Burri
on my left hand.
See, it doesn't take much and I'm off travelling again,
it's already a lot if poetry brings you
whenever you like
the time and strength to live for
just one moment. So come to bed, it's late.

(W.S. DiPiero)

Giro di macchina
di fronte all'estrema
finzione dell'estate
improvvisamente ripiombato
nell'alcova di carta
nell'ovattato silenzio:
tutto comincia
a riparlarmi di tutto,
dello zero assoluto.
Ripassa la macchina
e di colpo l'intero spazio
come un sipario si chiude
e si riapre da capo. Sono
continuamente distratto
da ciò che non accade.

(1982)

LUIGI FONTANELLA

Turning of the car
in front of the extreme
fiction of the summer
I'm suddenly sunk again
in the paper alcove
in the wadded silence:
everything begins again
to speak of everything,
of the absolute zero.
Now the car returns,
suddenly the whole space
closes like a curtain
and opens again. I am
continually distracted
by what doesn't happen.

(Michael Palma)

LUIGI FONTANELLA

MIMIKÒS

Ci sono disposizioni esatte
come quella della prima occhiata
corrisposte al taglio all'ondata e
la barca va in frantumi le scorie molli
schizzate nel cielo: testimone io
con le palme rimaste aperte
sul vetro dell'acquario.

(1982)

MIMIKÒS

There are exact arrangements
like that of the first glance
that correspond to the cut of the breakers and
the boat goes all to pieces the soft slag
splashed in the sky: I as witness
with my palms spread open
on the aquarium glass.

(Michael Palma)

LUIGI FONTANELLA

VICTORIA STATION

Si ammassavano volatili a scrosci di
risa e parole
                          un tumulto
per me viaggiatore ansioso del rientro...
tra fumo e orina incalzanti
corpi di donna intrecciati come alghe marine
soltanto sfiorate
                          io non amerò che te.

(1984)

VICTORIA STATION

The crowds amassed with sudden bursts of
laughter and words
                              a tumult
around me traveler anxious to get home...
amid smoke and urine pressing
bodies of women wreathing like seaweed
only grazing
                              I will love no one but you.

(Michael Palma)

LUIGI FONTANELLA

Sono in viaggio rettilineo col sole a picco
che gradualmente schioda e schianta e
squaglia la materia e di colpo
c'è la capra che bela il canto il coro ipnotico
l'erba che cresce che s'apre
a un grande solco fessura di carne
la tenera madre magma ribolle grassa
la mia testa è un profilo imprevisto:
passi di dea nascosta
che assorbe il filo degli anni.
Ricordo d'una passeggiata controtempo
a Capo Miseno (cosa vi cercavamo?),
adesso so che tutto comincia
da un errore o da un'imitazione.

(1984)

LUIGI FONTANELLA

I'm on a straight path with the sun gone down
that gradually dismantles smashes up and
melts away all matter and suddenly
there's the bleating goat the song the hypnotic chorus
the grass rising and opening up
to a wide furrow fissure of flesh
tender mother earth greasy boiling magma
my head is an unanticipated outline:
footsteps of the hidden goddess
who gathers the thread of the years.
A memory of a walk in the face of time
to Cape Miseno (what was I seeking there?),
now I know that everything begins
out of an imitation or a mistake.

(Michael Palma)

LUIGI FONTANELLA

L'immagine del lago ghiacciato
stamani ha figurato dal nulla
una giovane e bianca pattinatrice
poco lontano un vecchio in bicicletta
l'attraversava pian piano a tutto tondo: era
l'aprirsi lento d'un fiore
una rosa già frantumata in sabbia
il nano e la lucertola
immobili e attoniti
su un immenso sahara di ghiaccio.

(1984)

LUIGI FONTANELLA

The image of the frozen lake
has formed this morning out of nowhere
a young girl skating dressed in white
a little further an old man was riding
a bicycle in slow circles on the surface: it was
the gentle blossoming of a flower
a rose already shattered on the sand
the dwarf and the lizard
motionless and stunned
on a vast sahara of ice.

(Michael Palma)

LUIGI FONTANELLA

E'un tepore leggero che ritrovo
intatto e superbo in questo mattino
sbilenco. Ho pieni gli occhi d'un caleidoscopio:
è il passato presente
che m'inonda dentro. Tutto
si distende calmo ed esatto, qui
di fronte a questo lago, antico
come queste vette austere
che gli fanno corona.
Ogni attimo si perde e si rinnova altrove
un falso possesso la mia esistenza
sempre in fuga, io inseguitore inseguito,
e non so più se sto fuggendo da qualcosa
o rincorrendo una rosa
che dura lo spazio d'un solo mattino.

(1986)

LUIGI FONTANELLA

It's a slow warmth I find once more
intact and splendid on this stunted
morning. My eyes are filled with a kaleidoscope:
it's a past/present
flooding me within. Now everything
stretches out calmly and exactly, here
facing this lake, as old
as these austere peaks
ringing it with a crown.
Every moment is lost and somewhere else renewed
my existence a false possession
always in flight, I the pursuer pursued,
and I no longer know if I keep fleeing
from something, or keep seeking
a rose that lasts for the space of a single morning.

(Michael Palma)

LUIGI FONTANELLA

PADRE-SEQUENZA
per Gennaro Fontanella   (1911-1970)

1.

Mio padre ebbe molti amici nemici
ne ricordo uno in particolare di nome Grossi
soffriva anche lui d'ipertensione e di altri
        acciacchi, forse;
scimunito munito d'un sorriso melenso
ti parlava sempre di rimedi e medicine
da lui dottamente esperite
sottilmente compiacendosi, così,
di quest'amministrazione dell'altrui salute
e forse anche pensando meglio a te che a me:
ma poi anche lui morì.

2.

Stamattina ti ho improvvisamente riconosciuto
in una mia espressione casualmente
catturata allo specchio
in rimbalzo veloce atroce
nella sua nuda comunicazione: lo sguardo triste
sul tuo sorriso sempre ottimista.
Possibile che debba capirti meglio oggi
dopo quasi vent'anni trascorsi un po'
lontano, un po' solo, un po' egoista?

LUIGI FONTANELLA

FATHER-SEQUENCE
for Gennaro Fontanella   (1911-1970)

1.

My father had a lot of friendly enemies:
I especially remember one called Grossi
who also had hypertension and some other
     ailments, perhaps;
a runty monkey with a goofy smile
he was always talking to you about medicines
and remedies he, the authority, had tried,
taking a subtle satisfaction through
his management of other people's health
and perhaps even thinking, better him than me;
but then he died too.

2.

This morning I saw you suddenly
in one of my expressions casually
caught in the mirror
in a swift rebound, profoundly
shocked by its naked message: the sad cast
to your smile of the eternal optimist.
Can it be that I know you better now, having passed
nearly twenty years as a bit remote, a bit
alone with myself, a bit of an egotist?

3.

Mi scopro a ripensarti all'età mia di adesso
cogliendo con orrore la spietatezza del tempo
e la pochezza che mi resta, nel '54
con già quattro figli da sfamare partivi per il lavoro
ogni mattina in lambretta
senza cappotto
proteggendoti con fogli di giornale
che t'infilavi sotto la giacchetta.

4.

Troppo presto ci mancasti
e forse oggi sei stanco d'esser morto
ma vedi, or non è molto, da me promosso
ritornato appari in un altro volto
che ha un po' di te
e un po' di me addosso.

(1987)

LUIGI FONTANELLA

3.

I find myself thinking of you at the age I am now,
grasping with a shudder the ruthlessness of time
and the little I have left, in '54
already four children to feed you would leave for work
on your Lambretta every morning
without an overcoat
with the pages of newspapers stuffed
under your jacket, trying to keep warm.

4.

You went away from us too soon
and perhaps today you are tired of being dead,
but look, through what I have done, just recently
you appear to have returned in another face
that has a bit of you
in it, and a bit of me.

(Michael Palma)

LUIGI FONTANELLA

A EMMA

Prima che il sogno svanisca
piccola mia,
fa che quest'alba continui
infinita
fermotempo in questa pallida luce
nella quale infine t'addormenti
mentre io continuo stanco e svagato
a seguire l'incerta alternanza
tra sogno e veglia, o fantasia
che si posa leggera sui tuoi piccoli occhi
e per me è già nostalgia.

Prima che il sogno svanisca, bambina mia,
prendimi con la tua minuscola mano
insegnami a vivere senza pena o rimpianto
e senza paura
tu che, priva, dai forza con niente
tu forza di vita tu calamita
d'amore assoluta e imminente.

Prima che il sogno svanisca, piccola mia,
contiamo di quante perle
s'adorna questa bruna alcova
oggi rinata a misura. Ti seguo senza posa
mentre occhieggi curiosa al mondo

LUIGI FONTANELLA

FOR EMMA

Before the dream is gone
my little one
please let this dawn go on
forever
stilltime in this faint light
in which you fall asleep at last
while tired and distracted I go on
tracing the uncertain alternation
between dream and waking, a fantasy
gently alighting on your little eyes,
already a nostalgic dream for me.

Before the dream is gone, my little child,
take hold of me with your tiny hand
teach me to live without regret or pain
and without fear
you, helpless and with nothing, give me strength
you force of life, you magnet of
a love that is absolute and imminent.

Before the dream is gone, my little one,
we count how many pearls
adorn this dark alcove
now reborn in scale with you. I watch
transfixed as you glance curiously

che ti circonda. Cosa ci vedi?
Da quali segni iniziali sei attratta?
Chi sono? Chi sei?

Prima che il sogno svanisca
bambina mia, ti prego, fa che questa
mattina continui infinita
oltre l'incerta alternanza
fra sogno e veglia, o fantasia
che si posa leggera sui tuoi piccoli occhi
e per me è già nostalgia.

(1987-1988)

at the world encircling you. What do you see?
What holds your eye, where everything is new?
Who am I? Who are you?

Before the dream is gone
my little one, I beg you, please let this
morning go on forever
beyond the uncertain alternation
between dream and waking, a fantasy
gently alighting on your little eyes,
already a nostalgic dream for me.

(Michael Palma)

LA NOTTE QUALCUNO

La notte qualcuno al mio posto
si alza più di una volta
siccome vedo perfettamente nel buio
gli do istruzioni senza parlare
perché eviti scontri coi mobili
o con aguzze sporgenze.
Lui si muove cautamente
strusciando lieve i piedi per terra
evita la cassapanca dopo averne
tastato il legno della bordatura, sfiora
l'armadio con le dita,
ecco lo spigolo del comò
e la fugace carezza all'antiquata crespina
la falsa canadella il vecchio vaso di vetro
coi fiori secchi d'acetosella la culla di Emma e poi e poi.
E poi, ritornando al suo posto
scompare, buio nel buio
nero nel nero più cupo.

(1988)

LUIGI FONTANELLA

IN THE NIGHTTIME SOMEONE

In the nighttime someone in my place
arises more than once
since I can see perfectly in the dark
I give him instructions silently
lest he bump into the furniture
or up against sharp corners.
He moves cautiously, his feet
dragging softly over the ground
he inches around the chest after his hand
has probed its wooden trim, he grazes
the wardrobe with his fingertips,
here the corner of the bureau
and the feathery touch of the old-fashioned ruffle
the imitation antique pitcher the old glass vase
with dried sorrel flowers Emma's cradle and then,
    and then.
And then, returning to his place
he vanishes, dark in the dark
black in the deeper black.

(Michael Palma)

PATRIZIA CAVALLI

PATRIZIA CAVALLI

CRITICAL NOTE

Patrizia Cavalli was born in 1947 in Todi, in the central Italian region of Umbria. In 1968 she began her studies at the University of Rome, in which city she has lived ever since. She holds a baccalaureate in philosophy and an advanced degree in arts, with a thesis on the aesthetics of music. From an early age she has published her poetry widely in periodicals, and it has thus far been collected into two volumes, *Le mie poesie non cambieranno il mondo* (My Poetry Will Not Change the World 1974) and *Il cielo* (The Sky/Heaven 1981), both published by Einaudi. Her poems have also appeared in a number of anthologies. She has written two scripts for RAI (Radiotelevisione Italiana), *La bella dormentata* (Sleeping Beauty, 1979) and *Il guardiano dei porci* (The Swineherd, 1982). She has also been active as a translator of classic drama. Her verse translation of Molière's *Amphitryon* was published in 1981, and more recently she has translated two of Shakespeare's plays, *The Tempest* for the Gran Teatro of Florence in 1983 and *A Midsummer Night's Dream* for Milan's Teatro dell'Elfo in 1987.

Cavalli has made her way into the foreground of an Italian literary landscape still largely dominated, if not controlled, by men. This feat seems consistent with the self-confident persona that her poems project. Despite the claim that her poems "already don't resemble me/They've forgotten the anger/and the curse," both the anger and the curse can be felt beneath the sharp and often brittle surface. The "I" of these poems moves through a world of clear and brightly colored objects, preferring what can be touched. She seems too proud and self-contained to look for commitment in relationships, and yet relationships seem frequently to end in betrayal—if in no other way, then in the ultimate betrayal of death. Despite the defiance and the sensitivity to insult, there seems to be an acknowledgment (even perhaps a bit of cultivation) of vulnerability, but finally a refusal to submit to its seductions. Cavalli's poems are located in the physical world, but that world is perceived as alien and often threatening. Perhaps in part as a strategy for coping with such a world, the lines are hardedged and strong, and often a poem will end with a sudden turn of phrase or twist of thought that ties it off neatly. But in other poems, this turning brings us to a conclusion—an insight, a question, a teasing image—that lingers vividly in the mind.

—M.P.

POETRY

Le mie poesie non cambieranno il mondo. Turin, 1974.
Il cielo. Turin, 1981.

PATRIZIA CAVALLI

Qualcuno mi ha detto
che certo le mie poesie
non cambieranno il mondo.

Io rispondo che certo sì
le mie poesie
non cambieranno il mondo.

(1974)

Eternità e morte insieme mi minacciano:
nessuna delle due conosco,
nessuna delle due conoscerò.

(1974)

PATRIZIA CAVALLI

Someone told me
that of course my poetry
won't change the world.

I answer that of course not
my poetry
won't change the world.

(Judith Baumel)

Together eternity and death threaten me.
neither of the two do I know,
neither of the two will I know.

(Judith Baumel)

PATRIZIA CAVALLI

Di tutte le cacciatrici
la più bella. Una carta
di caramella come un uccellino
senza sangue. Ma lei sa
che l'omaggio è regale,
la cavaliera impunita.

(1974)

Prima quando partivi dimenticavi sempre
il tuo profumo, il fazzoletto più bello,
i pantaloni nuovi, i regali per gli amici,
i guanti, gli stivali e l'ombrello:
Questa volta hai lasciato
un paio di mutande
giallo portorico.

(1974)

PATRIZIA CAVALLI

Of all the huntresses
the most beautiful. A candy wrapper
like a bird
without blood. But she knows
that this is royal homage,
the unpunished lady-knight.

(Robert McCracken)

Before when you left you would always forget
your perfume, your best handkerchief,
your new pants, your gifts for friends,
your gloves, your boots and your umbrella.
This time you left
a pair of Puerto-Rico-yellow
underpants.

(Judith Baumel)

PATRIZIA CAVALLI

Non ho seme da spargere per il mondo
non posso inondare i pisciatoi né
i materassi. Il mio avaro seme di donna
è troppo poco per offendere. Cosa posso
lasciare nelle strade nelle case
nei ventri infecondati? Le parole
quelle moltissime
ma già non mi assomigliano più
hanno dimenticato la furia
e la maledizione, sono diventate signorine
un po' malfamate forse
ma sempre signorine.

(1974)

PATRIZIA CAVALLI

I have no seed to spread over the world
I can't flood urinals or
mattresses. My meager woman's seed
is too little to offend. What can I
leave in the streets, in houses,
in unfertilized bellies? Words
far too many
but they already don't resemble me
they've forgotten the anger
and the curse, they've become young ladies
with slightly bad reputations perhaps
but still young ladies.

(Robert McCracken)

PATRIZIA CAVALLI

Ma prima bisogna liberarsi
dall'avarizia esatta che ci produce,
che mi produce seduta
nell'angolo di un bar
ad aspettare con passione impiegatizia
il momento preciso nel quale
il focarello azzurro degli occhi
opposti, degli occhi acclimatati
al rischio, calcolata la traiettoria,
pretenderà un rossore
dal mio viso. E un rossore otterrà.

(1974)

I marocchini con i tappeti
sembrano santi e invece
sono mercanti.

(1974)

PATRIZIA CAVALLI

But first one must free oneself
of the precise greed that produces us,
that produces me sitting
in the corner of a bar
waiting with clerical passion
for the exact moment when
the little azure fires of the eyes
opposite, of the eyes acclimatized
to risk, the trajectory precalculated,
will demand a blush
from my face. And will obtain a blush.

(Robert McCracken and Patrizia Cavalli)

The Moroccans with the carpets
seem like saints
but they're salesmen.

(Kenneth Koch)

PATRIZIA CAVALLI

All'ombra di una metafora
datemi una margherita
perché io possa tenerla in mano
la margherita.

(1974)

Poco di me ricordo
io che a me sempre ho pensato.
Mi scompaio come l'oggetto
troppo a lungo guardato.
Ritornerò a dire
la mia luminosa scomparsa.

(1974)

PATRIZIA CAVALLI

In the shade of a metaphor
give me a daisy
that I may hold it in my hand
the daisy.

(Robert McCracken with Patrizia Cavalli)

Little of myself do I remember
I who always thought of myself.
I vanish from myself like an object
looked at for too long.
I will come back to tell
my luminous disappearance.

(Robert McCracken)

PATRIZIA CAVALLI

Quella nuvola bianca nella sua differenza
insegue l'azzurro sempre uguale:
lentamente si straccia nella trasparenza
ma per un po' mi consola del vuoto universale.
E quando cammino per le strade
e vedo in ogni passo una partenza
vorrei accanto a me un bel viso naturale.

(1981)

PATRIZIA CAVALLI

That white cloud in its contrast
chases the same constant blue.
Slowly it tears itself into transparency
but for a while it consoles me for the universal void.
And when I walk the streets
and see in every step a departure
I would like beside me a fine natural face.

(Judith Baumel)

PATRIZIA CAVALLI

Per simulare il bruciore del cuore, l'umiliazione
dei visceri, per fuggire maledetta
e maledicendo, per serbare castità
e per piangerla, per escludere la mia bocca
dal sapore pericoloso di altre bocche
e spingerla insaziata a saziarsi dei veleni del cibo
nell'apoteosi delle cene quando il ventre
già gonfio continua a gonfiarsi;
per toccare solitudini irraggiungibili e lí
ai piedi di un letto di una sedia
o di una scala recitare l'addio
per poterti escludere dalla mia fantasia
e ricoprirti di una nuvolaglia qualunque
perché la tua luce non stingesse il mio sentiero,
non scompigliasse il mio cerchio oltre il quale
ti rimando, tu stella involontaria,
passaggio inaspettato che mi ricordi la morte.

Per tutto questo io ti ho chiesto un bacio
e tu, complice gentile e innocente, non me lo hai dato.

(1981)

PATRIZIA CAVALLI

To simulate the burning of the heart, the humiliation
of the viscera, to flee cursed
and cursing, to horde chastity
and to cry for it, to keep my mouth
from the dangerous taste of other mouths
and push it unfulfilled to fulfill itself with the poisons of
food,
in the apotheosis of dinners when the already
swollen belly continues to swell;
to touch unreachable solitude and there
at the foot of a bed, a chair
or the stairs to recite a goodbye,
so that I can expel you from my fantasy
and cover you with ordinary clouds
so that your light will not fade my path,
will not muddle my circle from which
I send you, you unintentional star,
unexpected passage who reminds me of death.

For all this I asked you for a kiss
and you, kind and innocent accomplice, didn't give it to me.

(Judith Baumel)

PATRIZIA CAVALLI

Ah sí, per tua disgrazia,
invece di partire
sono rimasta a letto.

Io sola padrona della casa
ho chiuso la porta
ho tirato le tende.
E fuori i quattro canarini
ingabbiati sembravano quattro foreste
e le quattromila voci dei risvegli
confuse dal ritorno della luce.
Ma al di là della porta
nei corridoi bui, nelle stanze
quasi vuote che catturano
i suoni piú lontani
i passi miserabili di languidi ritorni
a casa, si accendevano nascite
e pericoli, si consumavano
morti losche e indifferenti.

E cosa credi che io non t'abbia visto
morire dietro un angolo
con il bicchiere che ti cadeva dalle mani
il collo rosso e gonfio
vergognandoti un poco
per essere stata sorpresa

PATRIZIA CAVALLI

Ah, yes, to your misfortune
instead of leaving
I stayed in bed.

I, sole mistress of the house,
closed the door,
drew the blinds.
And outside, the four caged
canaries sounded like four forests
and four thousand voices of reawakening
confused by the return of light.
But beyond the door
in the dark halls, in the nearly
empty rooms that capture
the furthest sounds,
the pitiful steps of languid homecomings,
births and hazards were kindled,
indifferent and furtive deaths
were consumed.

And what do you think, that I couldn't see you
die around a corner
with the glass falling from your hands
your neck red and swollen
a little ashamed
to have been surprised

ancora una volta
dopo tanto tempo
nella stessa posizione nella stessa condizione
pallida tremante piena di scuse?

Ma se poi penso veramente alla tua morte
in quale letto d'ospedale o casa o albergo,
in quale strada, magari in aria
o in una galleria; ai tuoi occhi che cedono
sotto l'invasione, all'estrema terribile bugia
con la quale vorrai respingere l'attacco
o l'infiltrazione, al tuo sangue pulsare indeciso
e forsennato nell'ultima immensa visione
di un insetto di passaggio, di una piega di lenzuolo,
di un sasso o di una ruota
che ti sopravviveranno,
allora come faccio a lasciarti andar via?

(1981)

PATRIZIA CAVALLI

yet another time
after so much time
in the same position, the same condition,
pale, trembling, filled with excuses?

But then if I really think about your death
in whatever house, hotel or hospital bed,
in whatever street, perhaps in air
or in a tunnel; about your eyes that surrender
to the invasion; about the ultimate terrible lie
with which you will want to repulse the attack
or the infiltration; about your blood pulsing hesitant
and frantic in the final immense vision
of a passing insect, of a fold in the sheet,
of a stone or a wheel
that will survive you
well then, how can I let you go away?

(Judith Baumel)

PATRIZIA CAVALLI

Lontano dai regni
come è ferma la stanza!
Vieni, respirami vicino,
che io scopra la dolcezza
di molte imperfezioni, qualche dente
in meno qualche ruga in più e il corpo
appena estenuato dalla noncuranza.

(1981)

Fingo di aspettarti per ingrandire i minuti.
E fai bene a non venire.

(1981)

PATRIZIA CAVALLI

Far from kingdoms
how steady is the room!
Come, breathe close with me
so I may discover the sweetness
of many imperfections, some missing
tooth, some extra wrinkle, and your body
worn out slightly by carelessness.

(Judith Baumel)

I pretend to wait for you to enlarge the minutes.
And you do well not to come.

(Judith Baumel)

PATRIZIA CAVALLI

Fuori in realtà non c'era cambiamento,
è il morbo stagionato che mi sottrae alle strade:
dentro di me è cresciuto e mi ha corrotto gli occhi
e tutti gli atri sensi: e il mondo arriva
come una citazione.

Tutto è accaduto ormai, ma io dov'ero?
Quando è avvenuta la grande distrazione?
Dove si è slegato il filo, dove si è aperto
il crepaccio, qual è il lago
che ha perso le sue acque
e mutando il paesaggio
mi scombina la strada?

(1981)

La pioggia mi riporta
i pezzi dispersi
degli amici, spinge in basso i voli
troppo alti, dà lentezza alle fughe e chiude
al di qua delle finestre finalmente
il tempo.

(1981)

PATRIZIA CAVALLI

Outside, in fact, there wasn't any change.
The ripened disease is what removes me from the streets:
It has grown inside me and corrupted my eyes
and all my other senses: and the world arrives
like a quotation.

Everything has happened by now, but me, but where was I,
when did the great diversion come,
where did the string become untied, where did the fissure
open up, which is the lake
that lost its waters
and, changing the landscape,
scrambles my way?

(Judith Baumel)

The rain brings me back
the dispersed pieces
of my friends, it presses down
flights too high, it slows down escapes and closes
on the side of the window, finally,
time.

(Judith Baumel)

Questa volta non lascerò che l'azzurro intravisto
e visto da dietro la finestra, dal margine di un tetto
all'altro, nell'unico grandioso spiegamento
della ripetizione, trasportando lo sguardo oltre
ogni limite oltre la visione delle distanze,
tentazione e ricatto di leggerezza e movimento,
  questa volta
non lascerò che mi corrompa nella promessa
  della luce.

Non lascerò che il volo degli odori, l'aria
sbattuta dai suoni e dalle ali, i rapidi baleni
di un piccione che si rispecchia nell'ombra
della grondaia, che ne ricama il bordo
passeggiando, che si getta nel vuoto per poi
risalire, mi trascinino nelle strade
per colpire il mio corpo, mutilo d'ogni
  geografia,
smemorato d'ogni inclinazione, per colpire
in me la piaga addormentata dello stupore.

(1981)

PATRIZIA CAVALLI

This time I won't permit the blue, glimpsed
and seen from behind the window, from the edge of
    one roof
to another, in the sole grand explanation
of repetition, carrying the glance beyond
every limit, beyond the vision of the distances,
temptation and blackmail of lightness and movement,
    this time
I won't permit it to bribe me in the promise of light.

I won't permit the flight of odors, the air
beaten by sounds and by wings, the fast flashes
of a pigeon mirrored in the shadow
of the eaves, that, walking, embroiders the edge,
that throws itself in the vacuum only to later
rise up, I won't permit them to drag me through the
    streets
to beat my body, defaced of all geography,
oblivious to all tendency, in order to beat
in me the sleeping wound of stupor.

(Judith Baumel)

PATRIZIA CAVALLI

Adesso che il tempo sembra tutto mio
e nessuno mi chiama per il pranzo e per la cena,
adesso che posso rimanere a guardare
come si scioglie una nuvola e come si scolora,
come cammina un gatto per il tetto
nel lusso immenso di una esplorazione, adesso
che ogni giorno mi aspetta
la sconfinata lunghezza di una notte
dove non c'è richiamo e non c'è piú ragione
di spogliarsi in fretta per riposare dentro
l'accecante dolcezza di un corpo che mi aspetta,
adesso che il mattino non ha mai principio
e silenzioso mi lascia ai miei progetti
a tutte le cadenze della voce, adesso
vorrei improvvisamente la prigione.

(1981)

PATRIZIA CAVALLI

Now that time seems all mine
and no one calls me for lunch or dinner,
now that I can stay to watch
how a cloud loosens and loses its color,
how a cat walks on the roof
in the immense luxury of a prowl, now
that what waits for me every day
is the unlimited length of a night
where there is no call and no longer a reason
to undress in a hurry to rest inside
the blinding sweetness of a body that waits for me,
now that the morning no longer has a beginning
and silently leaves me to my plans,
to all the cadences of my voice, now
suddenly I would like prison.

(Judith Baumel)

PATRIZIA CAVALLI

E rivedere la città e rivederla
come un villaggio domestico
tanta metropoli!

Né il vomito né lo strazio del treno sotterraneo
né la testa schiacciata dal sonno, l'avanzare di sciagura
e morte nello sputo nella tosse—l'invenzione assoluta
del vestito, il ricamo dei capelli—la spinta
lo schiaffo, il rumore gigante e segreto
come di un altro mondo e altrove—l'unico flutto
d'ogni suono senza riconoscimento e direzione—
le cacate dei cani anch'esse giganti, la luce
che confonde a ogni ora sempre che confonde
dritta negli occhi a frantumare
lo spettro; i bidoni i pidocchi, le case sventrate
la nuova vernice, la passeggiata misteriosa
e terribile, l'offesa dell'ultimo profumo per signora...

(1981)

PATRIZIA CAVALLI

And to see the city again and to see it again
like a village, familiar—
such a metropolis!

Not the vomit, not the havoc of the underground trains,
nor the head crushed by sleep, the advance of misfortune
and death in the spit of the cough; the total invention
of the clothes, the embroidery of the hair; the shove,
the slap, the noise, gigantic and secret
as from another world and elsewhere; the one single wave of
 every sound without recognition or direction—
the dogshit, also gigantic, the light
that confuses at every hour that always confuses
straight in the eyes to shatter
the spectrum, the trash cans, the lice, the ripped-out houses,
the fresh paint, the walk, mysterious and terrible,
the offense of the latest ladies' perfume...

(Judith Baumel)

PAOLO RUFFILLI

PAOLO RUFFILLI

CRITICAL NOTE

Born in 1949, Paolo Ruffilli attended the University of Bologna, where he studied modern literature. After a period of teaching high school, he became an editor with the Milanese publisher Garzanti, and is presently the general editor of Le Edizioni del Leone in Venice. As an editor, he has not only supported contemporary poetry but also shown a scholarly interest in the Italian literature of the nineteenth century, preparing editions of the *Operette morali* of Giacomo Leopardi, Ugo Foscolo's translation of Laurence Sterne's *Sentimental Journey*, and *Le confessioni d'un italiano* by the poet, novelist, and patriot Ippolito Nievo. Ruffilli has also written a biography of Nievo. He has published criticism in a number of periodicals, and is the regular literary critic of the Bolognese daily *Il Resto del Carlino*. Beginning in 1972, he has published six volumes of poetry, and has in preparation a further collection and a novel. His recent collection, *Piccola colazione* (1987), has been a tremendous success, selling more than five thousand copies in a nation where a sale of one thousand copies for a book of poems is considered quite healthy. The volume has won numerous prizes and was the subject of both a television special and a radio broadcast. An evening devoted to *Piccola colazione* was also held at the 1988 Frankfurt Book Fair, with papers read in Italian, French, German, Spanish, and English.

Piccola colazione is a thematically and stylistically linked volume of seven poems, a brief title poem followed by six extended ones, each prefaced by a pair of sharp epigraphs from writers

PAOLO RUFFILLI

as diverse as Swift, Proust, and Mishima. The six longer poems, of which "Malaria" is the first, form a kind of loose progression. Composed in short lines and irregular, mostly short stanzas, with recurring bursts of rhyme, they combine images, memories, narrative fragments, scraps of dialogue, and snatches of song, in what several commentators have described as an almost operatic technique. Ruffilli's style has been compared to the stream-of-consciousness method employed by Joyce and other novelists, the historical precedent for which is, interestingly, found in the works of Sterne. Ruffilli's techniques of dramatic collage also owe a great deal to Eliot and Pound. But, despite these influences, his style is both authentically original and unmistakably personal. Through associative and impressionistic methods, Ruffilli's poems build and sustain an intense atmosphere of fear, guilt, and desire. The *Frankfurter Allgemeine* describes *Piccola colazione* as "a coming-of-age novel in verse," and *Le Monde* calls it "one of the most important books of the last few years, destined to endure also as an *other* way of making poetry."

—M.P.

POETRY

La quercia della gazze. Forli, 1972.
Quattro quarti di luna. Forli, 1974.
Notizie dalle Esperidi. Forli, 1976.
Prodotti notevoli. Milan, 1980.
Piccola colazione. Milan, 1987.
Diario di Normandia. Montebelluna, 1990.

OTHER

Orfeo tra gli Argonauti: vita di Ippolito Nievo. Milan, 1984.

PAOLO RUFFILLI

MALARIA

Qual è più caro,
il nome o il corpo?
Lao-tzu

Il più alto grado di
presenza è l'assenza.
Walter Benjamin

«Troppo comodo
fare quello che piace
e che si vuole».

La scatola di latta
è tonda e ruota,
una parte sull'altra.
Si può odorarla, vuota,
e leccarla, quando
la liquerizia è terminata.

mela arancia susina
mela arancia susina

...da dove saltano

PAOLO RUFFILLI

MALARIA

Which is to be more prized,
the name or the body ?
Lao-tzu

The highest degree of
presence is absence.
Walter Benjamin

"It's too easy
doing what one likes
and what one wants."

The tin can
is round, and rolls,
one side over the other.
You can smell it, empty,
or lick it, when
the licorice is gone.

apple orange plum
apple orange plum

...from where they leap

fuori, i sogni,
vesti e contorni
al mostro, alla pazzia:
frullati, puzzle con
i tasselli fuori posto,
come uccelli colorati
o pipistrelli
staccatisi di colpo
dall' albero blu inchiostro.

«Dev'essere un accordo
dei grandi,
per dispetto o gelosia».

Sulla torre del castello
inespugnabile, sicura
da cui si tiene il resto
sotto mira. Un regno
piccolo ma certo, per
il tempo almeno in cui
la porta è chiusa a chiave.

(Scruta, salito
sul bordo della vasca

PAOLO RUFFILLI

out, dreams,
costumes and frills
monster-style, the madness:
milkshakes, puzzles
with pieces out of place,
like colored-in birds
or bats
flung suddenly
from the ink-blue tree.

"It must be an agreement
between grown-ups
out of spite or jealousy."

In the castle tower:
impregnable, secure
from which one holds the rest
in his sights. A tiny
kingdom, but dependable
at least as long as
the door is locked.

(He stares, perched
at the tub's edge

PAOLO RUFFILLI

in bilico, svestito,
indaga sullo specchio
la forma o una ragione
di tanto desiderio.)

pesa il passo e posa piano
lancia il sasso con la mano
ferma adesso o vai lontano

«Mia madre dice che
posso togliermi tutto».
«La mia, non più dei
pantaloni e della maglia».

(Vedersi, essere
visto. Metterlo a nudo.
Tenerlo, se deve essere
tenuto. Ma gli pare
che debba esserci
qualche altra cosa...)

Rosso. Di febbre, di
sangue. Dentro al fuoco.
Di unghie e labbra.
Di gente senzadio.
Di cappe, di bandiere.

and hovering, naked,
he studies the mirror,
his shape, the reason
for so much desire.)

judge your stride and easy stand
throw the stone with steady hand
stop now or go to a far-off land

"My mother tells me
I can take off everything."
"Mine says no more than
slacks and sweaters."

(To see oneself, to be
seen. To expose it, naked.
To hold it, if it has to be
held. But he thinks
there must be
something else.)

Red. Of fever, of
blood. In the fire.
Of nails and lips.
Of godless people.
Of cloaks, of banners.

PAOLO RUFFILLI

Nel sommergibile, «Io»,
in rotta per i mari.
«Tutti sottocoperta,
chiudere i boccaporti.
Immersione rapida».
Lo spazio circoscritto
la sacca degli odori
l'ombra del letto.

«...cuore, desco, nido
gnomo, soma, tetto».

Ancora. Esatta
la secca tiritera
parola per parola.
Specchio, ritratto
analogia, prova
che c'è, sotto, la cosa:
quel che sempre sarà
e sempre è stato,
non dovunque e
come sia. Dettato.

...sul *Libro dei*
Libri Famosi,
nell'enciclopedia.

PAOLO RUFFILLI

In the submarine, *Io*,
en route through the seas.
"Clear the deck.
Secure the hatch.
Dive, dive."
Cramped quarters
sackful of smells
shadow of the bed.

"...heart, table, nest,
gnome, bundle, home."

Again. Precise
the dry drawn out business
of word after word.
Mirror, portrait
analogy, proof
that there is, underneath, the thing:
that which always shall be
and always has been,
not wherever
as may be. Dictated.

...on *The Book
of Famous Books*
in the encyclopedia.

«...ha i colori
del fuoco, della neve
e del prato».

«Dai, paga il pegno.
Dire, fare, baciare,
lettera o testamento?».

(Non è che smetta
anzi, a rifarlo, gli
sembra anche più bello.
Però, ha il dubbio
che se resta magro
è proprio per quello.)

«Più vai veloce e
più, vedrai, ti piace».

...che una parola
abbia un sesso e una
persona (maschile se
finisce in *a*!). Ma
incomprensibile di più
lo stato di mancanza

PAOLO RUFFILLI

"...it has the colors
of fire, snow
and meadow."

"Come on, pay forfeit.
Speak, do, kiss,
letter or last will?"

(Not that he stops
redoing it, no,
it seems even better.
But he has the feeling
that if it stays half done
that is really why.)

"The faster you go the better
you like it, you'll see."

...that a word
have gender and
person (masculine
if ending in *a*!). But
more incomprehensible
the state of dearth

di assenza, insomma
la parvenza negata
in un concetto neppure
rifiutato, inconcepibile,
del *niente* e lo stupore
a pronunciarlo.

«La sua, dov'è?
Da cosa è fatta?».

(A lui il gusto, solo,
di essere preso. E
il pensiero che è
ingiusto e svantaggioso,
e non tanto per lei
in fondo, se non ce l'ha.)

«Lo imparerai, quando
sarai più grande».

Visto in segreto e detto
al chiuso, in ombra
bisbigli, incerti
i margini, mai esatti

PAOLO RUFFILLI

of absence, in short
the presence denied
in a concept not even
contested, inconceivable,
of *nothingness*, and
the amazement
of pronouncing it.

"Her own, where is it?
What is it made of?"

(For him, the pure relish
of being taken, and
the thought it is unjust,
disadvantageous,
and not so much for her,
in the end, if she hasn't got it)

"You'll understand it
when you grow up."

Glimpsed in secret, and uttered
in hiding, whispers
in the dark, shapes
uncertain, never clear

indizi di segnali
colti, strappati
in fretta e furia
a sillabe, per paura
di essere scoperti
prima di scoprire
centimetri quadrati
di anfratti, di peluria.

una rana nera e rara
sulla rena errò una sera

Paura che un vetro venga rotto
che il sale vada sparso
che si rovesci l'acqua mentre bolle
che una zingara entri in casa
che cada il fiasco d'olio
che si rovini la salute.
Paura di restare al buio
di trovare in casa un assassino
di cavarsi un occhio su una punta
di non essere promosso
di cadere in un burrone
di finire dentro a un lago
di annegare, di essere schiacciato.

PAOLO RUFFILLI

the evidence gathered, the clues,
snatched in haste
and frenzy,
in syllables, in fear
of being found out
before finding out
square indices
of recesses, soft hairs.

a frog a black one very rare
one night in the sand lost his bearing

Fear of a glass breaking
of salt spilling
of boiling water being turned over
of a gypsy getting into the house
of the flask of oil dropping
of ruining one's health.
Fear of being left in the dark
of finding a killer in the house
of scratching an eye on a point
of not being promoted
of falling in the ditch
of winding up in a lake
of being drowned, of being crushed.

PAOLO RUFFILLI

«...l'hai detto.
Già se l'hai pensato.
Che non sia stato,
non conta più».

«Ci stai, allora?
Dai, parliamo male».
«Dobbiamo dire
tutte parolacce».

Detti e guardati
sopra il dizionario.
Ammessi, dunque, o
non del tutto ignorati.
E gli altri, sinonimi
più amorfi e grigi,
almeno registrati.

«Si mettono così,
l'uno sull'altro».

(Sdraiato, a letto,
per l'ennesima prova
generale col cuscino.

PAOLO RUFFILLI

"...you said it.
Already had the thought.
That it didn't turn out
doesn't count."

"Will you join us, then?
Come on, let's talk dirty."
"We have to use
only bad words."

Said, and looked up
in the dictionary.
Words taken for granted
then, or not entirely ignored.
And those others, synonyms,
vaguer, clouded,
listed nonetheless.

"They arrange themselves this way,
one on top of the other."

(Stretched out in bed
for the nth time
rehearsing with the pillow.

PAOLO RUFFILLI

Febbrile e ansante
baciandolo, abbracciato.)

Contro lo specchio
rispetto a un altro,
piccolo, che scende e
sale, a controllare
qual è l'effetto
di una diversa visuale.

«Non devi stare
con certi mascalzoni».

Che sia davvero
proprio il tranello,
quello per tentarti
per farti cadere
e, preso nella rete,
condannato in eterno
tra urli e grida
nel lago, nella fossa
in mezzo al fuoco.

«Ciò che è confessato
è tolto. E resti libero
una volta assolto».

Fevered and panting,
kissing it, squeezing.)

In front of a mirror
facing another,
a small one, that
falls and rises to test
what the effect is
of different perspectives.

"You shouldn't hang around
bad characters."

Maybe in truth
the very snare
to draw you,
cause you to fall,
and, caught in the net,
doomed forever
amidst shouts and cries
in the lake, in the pit,
the middle of the fire.

"What is confessed
is taken away. You're free
once you're absolved."

(Lo tormenta, a un
tratto, l'idea sgomenta
di non rispondere affatto
al modello di purezza
cui l'hanno abituato.)

...che esca fuori
una bestemmia
senza volerlo, che
si formi in testa
per un innesco
incontrollato.

Ma, sì, chi è stato
ai sette primi venerdì
del mese, preghiere
e litanie per ogni sera,
qualunque cosa ha fatto
e che continua a fare
sicuramente è salvo.

«Intanto, dappertutto
Dio ti vede».

PAOLO RUFFILLI

(It torments him,
suddenly, the daunting idea
of not yielding entirely
to the model of purity
to which they have
conditioned him.)

...there issues forth
a curse
without his thinking it,
as if lodged in his head
like a fuse
accidentally tripped.

But of course whoever
attends the first seven
Fridays of the month,
prayers and litanies every
evening,
whatever he has done
or keeps doing,
he is certainly saved.

"Meanwhile, everywhere,
God watches you."

PAOLO RUFFILLI

(Punta là, senza
saperlo. È attratto
per istinto, risucchiata
la sua mano, intanto,
a quel convesso
senza appiglio.)

«Lo dico a tua madre
che mi tocchi».

...che accada e
non importa come,
che finalmente
sia tolta ogni riserva
e, costi quel che costi,
si abbia il seguito.
Nonostante l'idea
magari di disgusto,
anche nel sangue
nel puzzo e nel sudore.

«Piace anche a lei,
non credere».

PAOLO RUFFILLI

(He points there,
without being aware.
He is pulled as by instinct,
at the same time
his hand swallowed up
in that convexity,
nothing to hold on.)

"I'm going to tell your mother
you touch me."

...that it may happen,
it doesn't matter how,
that at last
stripped of all scruples,
whatever the cost,
you're left with the outcome.
Notwithstanding even
thoughts of disgust,
even the blood,
stink, sweat.

"She likes it too,
not to believe."

PAOLO RUFFILLI

Da consumarsi in fretta
al buio, al chiuso
della stanza,
senza che si veda o
che si senta, di nascosto
di straforo, a danno
di qualcuno, come offesa
rischio e, più, vergogna
violando, meglio che
si possa, la consegna.

...ed è, risulta
inconsistente,
quanto più detto
ordinato e richiesto,
contro lo stare
fermo e sordo, questo
sì imperioso e urgente,
del suo nome.

Di nuovo ripetuto
tra sé o a voce alta
riscritto in lunghe
file sui quaderni,

PAOLO RUFFILLI

To spend oneself in haste,
in the dark, the secrecy
of the room,
without being seen
or heard, hiding,
on the sly, in danger
from all, offense,
risk, even more, shame,
violating—as hard
as he can—a trust.

...and it is, it proves
insubstantial,
the more it is claimed
as ordained, commanded
—this thing so imperious
and pressing—
against his good standing,
and scornful of his good name.

Once more, repeating
to himself, or out loud,
putting it down again
long lines in notebooks,

in grande e in piccolo
corsivo o stampatello
in alfabeto greco
con la grafia più antica
disegnato, perfino
cesellato. Sempre quello.

«A una cui vuoi bene
non lo fai.»

Che sia dannata, sì,
e impura e lurida
perduta... ma destinata
a spegnere una sete
appetitosa, proprio
per questa cosa,
dolorosamente desiderata.

(Il sogno suo è di
perdersi, di cadere tra
le mani di una donna
senza scrupoli.)

PAOLO RUFFILLI

capital letters or small,
hand-written, printed
in the Greek alphabet
in the oldest style
devised, even carved,
as with a chisel.
Always the same thing.

"You don't do that
to a girl you like."

Yes, let her be damned,
corrupt and a scandal,
forsaken... but destined
to slake a growing
thirst, for this
one thing
such dolor, such desire.

(He dreams
of losing himself, of
falling
into the hands of a
woman
without scruples.)

PAOLO RUFFILLI

«Si fanno fare
quello che ti pare.»

Da compitare, legato
a un altro, spingendo
sui contorni, a voce quasi
spenta, smozzicata
sotto ai denti come
sotto la sottana,
il soffio disperato
di... *puttana*.

(1987)

PAOLO RUFFILLI

"Things turn out
the way you think."

To spell it out, clasped
to another, straining
to the limit, voice almost
spent, stifled
by clenched teeth, as
under the skirt
the desperate sigh
of... *whore.*

(Felix Stefanile)

PAOLO RUFFILLI

S PECCHIO   CONFIDENTE

«...perchè, per
certe cose, non
serve la testa.»

l'istinto primitivo
il genio della specie
l'urlo della foresta

La camera da letto
è ingombra e
zigzagante, per chi
ci cammina, tagliata
tutta di sbieco e
confinante con la cucina.

(Un sovrapporsi di
pensieri, anticipando
le emozioni, gli atti
minimi, le azioni: il
rimescolarsi nel più
fondo dei suoi
visceri—la preda
già agognata—.

PAOLO RUFFILLI

PERSONAL MIRROR

"...because, in
certain things, the head
is of no use."

primitive instinct
the genius of the species
the howl of the forest

The bedroom
is cluttered and
zigzagging, for who
walks through, spilling
disorder all over and
adjoining the kitchen.

(An overlapping of
one's thoughts, anticipating
the emotions, the least
gestures, the movements: the
churning
deep in the gut—the prey
coveted once more—

Con lei che si avvicina
mascherata.)

Nella stanza chiusa
arresa segregata
perduta sul filo della
mente, sprofondata
nel sé di sé
contratta arresa
sbottonata. La cosa
vergognosa, l'amante
sua, la sposa.

«Lo sai, che
no, non vale.»
«Però io, sì,
ti amo.»

Sfiorato avvolto
blandito imprigionato,
specchio confidente
alimento prepotente
ossigenato, l'essere
amato, preteso e
dichiarato.

PAOLO RUFFILLI

for her who approaches,
masked.)

In the closed room
sealed off as it were
astray on the mind's
track, plunged
into the inmost self
bound delivered
laid bare. The shameful
fact, his lover,
the bride.

"You know, of course,
it's not worth it."
"But for me, yes,
I love you."

Brushed lightly turned over
preened over imprisoned,
personal mirror,
strong nutrient,
oxidized, the being
loved, claimed
and spoken for.

PAOLO RUFFILLI

infine, giacendo
distesa: l'ho
presa, l'ho presa...

(Lui non l'ha, però,
amata. Si illude
di averla, almeno,
tenuta. La parte
cruda, non certo
quella buona.)

Ombrosa e mora,
la signora sofisticata:
schiava e padrona
di un sogno, dell'idea
di consegnarsi alla
condanna del piacere.

(1989)

PAOLO RUFFILLI

In the end, she lying down
supine: I took her,
I took her.

(He has not, however,
loved her. He deludes himself
that at least
he has held her. The raw
deed, and for sure
not the best part.)

Nervous, delaying,
the lady sophistical
slave and master
of a dream, of the idea
of giving herself up
to the sentence of pleasure.

(Felix Stefanile)

MILO DE ANGELIS

MILO DE ANGELIS

CRITICAL NOTE

Born in Milan in 1951, Milo De Angelis spent his childhood in the Piedmontese village of Monferrato. Athletic in his youth, he played soccer as well as competing in track and field. He studied classics at universities in Italy and France, and later worked as a private tutor in Latin and Greek. In 1975, after he had been writing poetry for about ten years, he achieved a breakthrough debut when his work appeared in two influential anthologies and was favorably noticed by the poet Franco Fortini. In the following year he published his first book of poems, *Somiglianze* (Resemblances). This book has been followed by three subsequent collections, a volume of critical essays, a prose narrative, and several translations from French and Latin. A frequent traveler and occasional resident abroad, De Angelis now lives in the city of his birth.

De Angelis' poetry is undeniably difficult—rigorous in its execution and severe in its demands upon the reader's concentration. It is a body of work strikingly distinguished by its unity, intensity, and philosophical foundations. A De Angelis poem is typically short and short-lined, showing even in its appearance on the page the Hermetic influence upon his development. Stylistically, it is precisely controlled, especially at the level of the individual image. Recurring patterns of imagery—the cycle of the seasons, for example—thread their way through the body of his work. But these images are set discretely in a pattern of abrupt juxtapositions and swift associational leaps, transcending logic and order. "For De Angelis,"

MILO DE ANGELIS

says Lawrence Venuti, who has been studying and translating De Angelis almost since the beginning of the poet's public career, "the function of poetry is to stimulate originary thinking by pushing at the limits of language and transgressing cultural norms, but always with the awareness that their destruction is simultaneously tragic and creative, the end of existence and the ceaseless proliferation of new beginnings." The reader who comes to this poetry with openness and sensitivity will be impressed by its integrity, stirred by its striking and often quite beautiful phrasing, and moved by feelings and insights that, however ineffable, are genuine and profound.

—M.P.

POETRY
Somiglianze. Milan, 1976.
Millimetri. Turin, 1983.
Terra del Viso. Milan, 1985.
Distante un padre. Milan, 1989.

OTHER
La corsa dei mantelli (narrative). Milan, 1979.
Poesia e destino (essays). Bologna, 1982.

MILO DE ANGELIS

I SUONI GIUNTI

Il lupo è ancora sotto la coperta
e occorrono mille domande per capirlo
anche se la voglia
è di credere subito a tutto
pronunciando un grazie silenzioso e intenso
l'unità della sabbia, la mano destra che tocca
la sinistra luminosa delle statue egiziane
una calma che resta,
rifiorisce nel rito, questo giugno
di una preghiera esaudita
la maestra, le scale
e nel grembo c'è il colore dei capelli
e poi il minuto d'oro,
il verde scuro del limone.

(1976)

MILO DE ANGELIS

THE SOUNDS THAT ARRIVED

The wolf is still under the blanket
and a thousand questions are needed to grasp it
even if the desire
is to believe in everything at once
uttering a quiet, intense thanks
the unity of the sand, the right hand touching
the luminous left on the Egyptian statues
a calm that remains,
blooms again in the rite, this June
it's an answered prayer
the schoolmistress, the little stairs
the hair color is in the womb
and then the golden instant,
the lemon's dark green.

(Lawrence Venuti)

MILO DE ANGELIS

ALLORA L'ACQUA

Anche nella mietitura
il corpo era solo imprestato
perché voleva diventare
innocente alla fine

e correndo
non rinunciava
a un'antologia dei gesti

il corpo esile
entrando nella stanza della principessa
per amare la prima volta.

(1976)

MILO DE ANGELIS

AND THEN THE WATER

In the harvest too
the body was only lent
because it wanted to become
innocent in the end

and running
it didn't renounce
an anthology of gestures

the slender body
entering the princess's room
to love the first time.

(Lawrence Venuti)

MILO DE ANGELIS

ORA C' È LA DISADORNA

Ora c'è la disadorna
e si compiono gli anni, a manciate,
con ingegno di forbici e
una boria che accosta
al gas la bocca
dura fino alla sua spina
dove crede
oppure i morti arrancano verso un campo
che ha la testa cava
e le miriadi
si gettano nel battesimo
per un soffio.

(1983)

MILO DE ANGELIS

NOW SHE IS UNADORNED

Now she is unadorned
and the years come to pass, in handfuls,
with the wit of shears and
an arrogance that draws
to the gas the mouth
persistent down to the spine
where it believes
or else the dead trudge toward a field
that has a hollow head
and the myriads
hurl themselves into the baptism
for a breath.

(Lawrence Venuti)

MILO DE ANGELIS

NEI POLMONI

La coperta, la sua forza, mentre crescevamo.
O gli occhi che ieri furono ciechi,
oggi tuoi, ieri l'inseparabile. Le fiale,
il riso in bianco diventano l'unico
mondo senza simbolo. Materia che
fu soltanto materia, nulla che
fu soltanto materia. Vegliare, non vegliare, poesia,
cobalto, padre, nulla, pioppi.

(1985)

MILO DE ANGELIS

IN THE LUNGS

The blanket, its weight, while we were growing.
Or the eyes, which yesterday were blind,
today yours, yesterday the indivisible. The vials,
the laughter in white becomes the only
world without symbol. Matter that
was only matter, nothing that
was only matter. Watch, don't watch, poetry,
cobalt, father, nothing, poplars.

(Lawrence Venuti)

ANNO

Scavando
verso un estremo di quaresima
sono stato spinto
dal seme. Mezzogiorno
che nel suo ordine si rovescia.
D'istinto puro, ogni volta, era
la mano fermata logicamente
tra gli agguati
di quell'età o il dolore di mia madre
non c'ero, non sceglievo. Dal citofono
esce colore mentale
dove l'uomo è nudo.
Quella goccia
vista nelle tre metà
diventò l'unica sostanza esterefatta, un
fervore di secoli...
...ogni pino...ogni pino...fermati,
tu sei fra di te.
Ruote che si sottraggono lentamente
al gelo, umiltà di una porta.

(1989)

MILO DE ANGELIS

YEAR

Digging
toward a Lenten extreme
I was pushed
by the seed. Noon
overturned in its order.
Instinctively pure, every time, was
the hand stopped logically
between the snares
of that age and my mother's pain
I wasn't there, I didn't choose. The intercom issues
mental color
where the man is naked.
That drop
seen in three shares
became the only terrified substance, a
centuries-old ardor...
every pine tree...every pine...stop,
you are amid yourself.
Wheels withdrawing slowly
from the ice, a door's humility.

(Lawrence Venuti)

MILO DE ANGELIS

RIGA

Alla testa ondeggiante nel mirino
preferimmo una
malattia di gradi freddi e sottrazioni: è
odio anch'essa, lo so, ma questo
fuscello si fa idea inseguendola per
un anno di limbo. E noi, applausi
scoloriti, abitammo la notte,
la sfuggente, meravigliosa pedana. Penetrazione
di sole in grano, che è madre. Superstite
che si chiama padre.

(1989)

MILO DE ANGELIS

LINE

To the head bobbing in the gunsight
we preferred an
illness of cold degrees and withdrawals: this too is
hate, I know, but this
twig turns idea pursued for
a year in limbo. And we, applause
faded, inhabited the night,
the elusive, marvelous springboard. Penetration
of sun in grain, which is mother. Survivor
whose name is father.

(Lawrence Venuti)

TELEGRAMMA

La finestra è rimasta come prima. Il freddo
ripete quell'essenza idiota di roccia
proprio mentre tremano le lettere di ogni parola.
Con un mezzo sorriso indichi
una via d'uscita, una scala qualunque.
Nemmeno adesso hai simboli per chi muore.
Ti parlavo del mare, ma il mare è pochi
    metri quadrati,
un trapano, appena fuori. Era anche, per noi,
l'intuito di una figlia che respira
nei primi attimi di una cosa. Carta per dire
brodo e riso, mesi per dire cuscino. Gli azzuri
    mi chiamano
congelato in una stella fissa.

(1989)

MILO DE ANGELIS

TELEGRAM

The window remained as before. The cold
repeats that idiotic essence of rock
just as the letters of every word tremble.
With a half smile you point
out an exit, some stairs.
Not even now have you symbols for the dead.
I spoke to you of the sea, but the sea is a few
        square meters,
a drill, scarcely out. It was also, for us,
the intuition of a daughter breathing
in the first moments of a thing. Paper to say
broth and rice, months to say pillow. The blue ones
        call me
frozen in a fixed star.

(Lawrence Venuti)

MILO DE ANGELIS

PROTEGGIMI MIO TALISMANO

Marta abbiamo trovato la cassetta
che un mattino nascose nella sabbia,
nell'orto, nella tastiera, marta
una figura umana non ultimata porta
quello che resta del suo accento, ma
domandava sempre verso un vetro, ma
non c'eravamo e il vestito cadde
sull'asfalto marta c'era un segno di
scarlattina dove inizia il petto, la
doppia giustizia, il doppio abitacolo,
la madre di piuma che noi lasciamo.

(1989)

MILO DE ANGELIS

PROTECT ME, MY TALISMAN

Marta we found the little box
that one morning she buried in the sand,
in the garden, in the keyboard, marta
an unfinished human figure carries
what remains of her accent, but
she always asked facing a window pane, but
we weren't there and the dress fell
to the asphalt marta there was a mark from
scarlet fever where the chest begins, the
double justice, the double cage,
the feathered mother we leave.

(Lawrence Venuti)

MILO DE ANGELIS

«VERSO LA MENTE»

Prima che dormissero le mirabelle
e la vera carta diventasse cieca
indietreggiò sentendosi
colpita e non riconobbe
il cane nell'acqua...
era suo padre...
corse via dalla cucina
fece un cenno
dove capitò il cielo
stracciando la carta carbone
lavando i bicchieri con la cenere
anatre come patriarchi
sorvegliano che tutto sia in ordine
tirò fuori il costume da bagno
e lo mostrò alla notte
bilance rincorrono bilance
la benda odora forte di
zuppa di pesce
e il grembiule è rinchiuso nella testa:
attese sul platano che
un lungo pensiero finisse
poi si affacciò alla finestra

MILO DE ANGELIS

"ON THE WAY TO MIND"

Before the plums fell asleep
and the true paper turned blind
she withdrew feeling herself
struck and didn't recognize
the dog in the water...
it was her father...
he ran away from the kitchen
nodded
where the sky arrived
ripping the carbon paper
washing the glasses with ash
ducks like patriarchs
see that everything is in order
she pulled out her bathing suit
and showed it to the night
scales chase scales
the bandage has a strong odor of
fish soup
and the apron is locked inside her head:
she waited on the plane tree for
a long thought to end
then looked out the window

e mentre l'erba aspettava
erano passati nove giorni di
giugno.

(1989)

MILO DE ANGELIS

and while the grass was waiting
nine days passed in
June.

(Lawrence Venuti)

IL NARRATORE

Giudice di un sasso abnorme,
al caldo dei moli, al freddo
degli olmi. Lentamente
gira il polso
tra laser e dolci nomi di albicocca
anch'io abito in questa porta girevole
scorrendo la colonna degli annunci
con pitture in affitto, gatti regalati,
busso a questo culto ebete,
insegnando l'alfabeto con la stessa fantasia
che mi oscura l'altra parte.

(1989)

MILO DE ANGELIS

THE NARRATOR

Judge of an abnormal stone,
in the heat of the piers, in the cold
of the elms. Slowly
the wrist turns
between the laser and sweet names for apricot
I too inhabit this revolving door
scouring the classified columns
with paintings for rent, cats given away,
I knock this obtuse cult,
teaching the alphabet with the same imagination
that obscures the other side to me.

(Lawrence Venuti)

IL PROGRAMMA DI HILBERT

I

Siamo caduti sulla sedia
per un movimento sbagliato della biro
aggrappandoci alla grazia,
alla nostra grazia annerita di tabacco.
Siamo caduti sul balcone
da cui gettavano sale. Ultraterrena,
una sostanza congiunta all'uovo
scruta i tempi finali dell'ossigeno.

II

Sulla destra la nostra
firma che ci torna contro. Sulla sinistra
un sirventese a punta secca:
«tua figlia, viva, prenderà l'anima
alla mia che muore.»
I ballerini ci chiamano
nel corpo sottostante, hanno
un tacere e un voltarsi
matita d'erba nella matita alta.

MILO DE ANGELIS

HILBERT'S PROGRAM

I

We fell on the chair
through a mistaken movement of the pen
clinging to grace,
our tobacco-stained grace.
We fell on the balcony
where they threw salt. Ultraearthly,
a substance joined to the egg
scrutinizes the last days of oxygen.

II

On the right our
signature turning against us. On the left
a sirvente with a dry-point:
"your daughter, alive, will assume the soul
of mine, who is dying."
The dancers call us
in the body below, they have
a silence and a turning
pencil of grass in the tall pencil.

III

Interi ripiani, pieni di oggetti, crollarono
nella banca. Rivedo quella scena:
la gente ammutolita, la celere,
gli angoli e il filo rovente, strano rondò
di una parola
al culmine della luce e della gola
«...ogni pino...ogni pino...fermati,
     tu sei fra di te...»

IV

Così facemmo nostro il rimorso di
ogni ladro; indiziati,
abbiamo vissuto d'incenso
dietro il cristallo del gineceo
fissiamo l'assoluta metà
di una cosa, un alimento
ripetuto a decenni, chiuso nel midollo
raccogliendo per terra pianeti
della fortuna, scatolette per gatti
che anche aperte ci danno un confine.

MILO DE ANGELIS

III

Interior shelves, full of objects, collapse
in the bank. I see that scene again:
the dumbstruck people, the fast ones,
the corners and the scorching wire, strange rondo
of a word
at the climax of light and throat
"every pine tree...every pine...stop,
         you are amid yourself..."

IV

Thus we made ours the remorse
of every thief; suspected,
we lived on incense
behind the crystal in the gynaeceum
we stare at the absolute middle
of a thing, a nutriment
repeated for decades, enclosed in the marrow
gathering on the ground fortune-telling
leaflets, little boxes for cats
which even when open set a limit for us.

MILO DE ANGELIS

V

Oscillano le corde dell'ascensore, ogni cosa
è divisa in memoria e mandragola.
Prima il ballo con la neve. Poi le processioni
del riposo come un capolavoro
da cui uscire scalzi. «Nell'acqua
a chi tace non si perdona.»
Nell'ora di un quaderno, io risposi,
　　　se furono chiamati lì,
è stato per un serio inferno, per un gioco letterario
che talvolta i suicidi hanno.
Quante borracce regalate
prima di affogare, quanta terra
sparsa sul cuscino!

VI

Stringevo forte l'idea: e allora nozze.
Salivo in fretta al quinto piano: e allora ho udito.
Tu che dicevi: addio passioni
di vita allucinata, voglio accendere
una lampada, svegliarmi qui, sentire
passi leggeri sulle mani.
Il giorno è quella donna che
allatta contro il muro, quello zen

MILO DE ANGELIS

V

The elevator cables sway, every thing
is divided into memory and mandrake.
First the dance with the snow. Then the processions
of repose like a masterpiece
whence to venture out barefoot. "In the water
whoever is silent isn't forgiven."
In the hour of a notebook, I answered,
    if they were called there,
it was for some serious hell, a literary game
suicides sometimes play.
How many canteens given away as presents
before drowning, how much earth
spread on the pillow!

VI

I squeezed the idea hard: and then marriage,
I rushed up to the fifth floor: and then I heard.
You were saying: goodbye passions
of hallucinated life, I want to light
a lamp, to wake up here, to feel
soft steps over my hands.
The day is that woman who
nurses against the wall, that zen

appoggiato. Tu che dicevi:
ho guardato la riga tra i capelli, sono
tornata sul lucernaio, per i saggi.

Noi bambini, noi aghi di pini.

VII

«Qui l'acqua non ritorna, la ritrovi in una gola.»
A ogni giro della terra,
lo stesso viso. Nessun crepaccio
è profondo come quelle rughe. «Sì, possiamo
scambiare la mia vita con la tua, se lo vuoi.»
Testavela, ti chiamavo. Su un vecchio scivolo
dormivi ancora, traballi un po',
disegni un nove e mezzo al corpo libero.
Aspro chiedere
è il segno dei gemelli...la figlia migrante,
la taciturna delle colline: poi il polline
entrò nei morti e un pranzo apparve
al buio, di amici.
Era ancora lì,
a dicembre, ed era la stessa, potevamo riconoscerla.

(1989)

MILO DE ANGELIS

leaning. You were saying:
I looked at the part in my hair, I
turned back to the oil lamp, for the sages.

We children, we pine needles.

VII

"The water doesn't come back here, you find it
        again in a throat."
At every turn of the earth,
the same face. No fissure
is as deep as those wrinkles. "Yes, you can
exchange my life for yours, if you want."
Head-sail, I called you. On an old slipway
you still sleep, stagger a little,
draw nine and a half meters with a free body.
Harsh begging
is the sign of twins...the migrating daughter,
the taciturn one from the hills: then the pollen
entered the dead and a supper appeared
in the dark, with friends.
She was there again,
in December, and it was the same one,
        we could recognize her.

(Lawrence Venuti)

INTUIZIONE FINITA

Un nervo ruota e quello spazio
cerca un graffio nella colla,
il punto fuori pagina

«La terra che fai rotolare
dov'è?»

Ti porterò a spalla,
cremazione perfetta e circondata da pali:
più degli angeli sono segreti i suicidi
e dal lato senza buio
la nuca cucita darà principio
al principio

Ti porterò a spalla, a stracci, a
leggere, oltre il muro, oltre quelli

«Il corpo era assiderato,
purpureo, privo di essenza.»

(1989)

MILO DE ANGELIS

FINITE INTUITION

A nerve pivots and that space
seeks a scratch in the glue,
point outside page

"Where's
the earth you send spinning?"

I shall carry you on my shoulders,
complete cremation surrounded by posts:
suicides are more secretive than angels
and from the darkless side
the stitched nape will begin
the beginning

I shall carry you on my shoulders, in tatters, to
read, beyond the wall, beyond those

"The body was frost-bitten,
purple, devoid of essence."

(Lawrence Venuti)

REMO NEL GENNAIO CONOSCIUTO

Lo seppi da un amico: sposi. Lei più anziana
con un piccolo albergo a Macerata,
lui aperto in una crepa bianchissima. Nella lettera
parlava dei filtri con cui d'inverno
si misura il sangue. Ricordo il cellofan sporco,
la mano dentro i vetri. Un alfabeto stride
nascosto tra dolci chiglie capovolte e
foto-tessera. *C'è un amore più grande*
di te e di me, me e voi nella specie,
acqua su acqua.

(1989)

MILO DE ANGELIS

ROWING IN FAMILIAR JANUARY

I knew him as a friend: married. She was older
had a little hotel in Macerata,
he was open in the whitest fissure. In the letter
he spoke of filters to measure the blood
in winter. I remember the dirty cellophane,
the hand behind the glass. An alphabet creaks
hidden among the smooth overturned keels and
the photo-I.D. *There is a love greater*
than you and me, me and you in the species,
water over water.

(Lawrence Venuti)

MILO DE ANGELIS

ANNUARIO

Dal corpo spinato, fili
si arrampicano in aria
con la prova dell'urlo. Come una
primitiva formula di povertà,
tutto il cibo si scioglie
nelle gocce per il cuore, tutto il sonno
s'incrosta alla materia, quell'incontro
tra raptus e firmamento
dove ritorniamo cancellati.

(1989)

MILO DE ANGELIS

YEARBOOK

From the barbed body, wires
climb into the air
with the proof of a scream. Like a
primitive formula of poverty,
every meal melts
into drops through the heart, every sleep
is encrusted in matter, that meeting
between raptus and firmament
from which we return erased.

(Lawrence Venuti)

MILO DE ANGELIS

TEMPO CONTINUATO

Ci ha consegnato
poche scatole, identiche,
piene di latte, di nessuna maternità.
Sono allarme e completezza,
sono rottami. Nell'ora di un quaderno, questo
quaderno essiccato. «Non mi trovano
gli occhi.» Allarme e completezza.
    Di colui
che ci accompagnò sulla terraferma
tutti noi serbiamo lo stile.

(1989)

MILO DE ANGELIS

CONTINUOUS TIME

We were consigned
little boxes, identical,
filled with milk, from no maternity.
They are warnings and completeness,
they are scraps. In the hour of a notebook, this
desiccated notebook. "The eyes
don't find me." Warnings and completeness.
    Of the one
who accompanied us on terrafirma
we all preserve the style.

(Lawrence Venuti)

VALERIO MAGRELLI

VALERIO MAGRELLI

CRITICAL NOTE

Valerio Magrelli was born in Rome in 1957. He studied literature and philosophy, an intertwining of interests that one sees reflected in his mature poetic style. Magrelli began publishing in 1977. His early work appeared in a number of leading journals, such as *Nuovi Argomenti* and *Periodo Ipotetico*, and was included in several influential anthologies, most notably Antonio Porta's *Poesia degli anni settanta* (1979). From the beginning Magrelli's work was recognized as especially accomplished, and many critics consider him the most promising poet of his generation. Over the past decade, Magrelli has published articles and reviews in weekly and daily newspapers. At present he writes regularly for *Il Messaggero*. A trained linguist, Magrelli has been quite active as a translator, publishing in both periodicals and books his versions mainly from the French (Verlaine, Stendhal, Mallarmé, Valéry, Vian, and others). Magrelli has published two collections of his own poetry, each of which has won a major award. The Premio Mondello went to *Ora serrata retinae* in 1980, and *Nature e venature* (1987), received the highly prestigious Premio Viareggio. He lives in Rome with his wife and young son.

Magrelli's poetry combines cool intellectualism with intense but understated emotion. The poems often begin with the careful examination of an object or environment which the speaking voice matter-of-factly describes in a way which betrays its

VALERIO MAGRELLI

subjective importance. Magrelli frequently achieves his characteristic effect of involuntary disclosure by piling one suggestive metaphor on another until the presumed object of discussion is surrounded by an electric aura of emotional association. Although the real subject of the poem is usually left unstated, Magrelli's deft exposition leaves its emotional importance unambiguous. The exceptional beauty of Magrelli's poetry comes from both the stunning originality of his metaphors and the subtle counterpoint he creates between secrecy and revelation. Magrelli also delights in irony. The more emotional his subject matter, the more coldly analytical his approach; the more intellectual his topic (as in his many poems on writing poetry), the more earthy his treatment. His style is concise and elegantly unadorned, but the language is supercharged to capture every nuance. While there is usually a touch of dry humor in his poems, the subjects they discuss—love, loss, creativity, and introspection—are never trivialized. In an utterly modern way Magrelli has revivified the traditional dialectic between body and soul, intellect and emotion, desire and achievement which has distinguished Italian lyric poetry since Dante and Petrarch.

—D.G.

POETRY

Ora serrata retinae. Milan, 1980.
Nature e venature. Milan, 1987.

VALERIO MAGRELLI

Domani mattina mi farò una doccia
nient'altro è certo che questo.
Un futuro d'acqua e di talco
in cui non succederà nulla e nessuno
busserà a questa porta. Il fiume
obliquo correrà tra i vapori ed io
come un eremita siederò
sotto la pioggia tiepida,
ma né miraggi né tentazioni
traverseranno lo specchio opaco.
Immobile e silenzioso, percorso
da infiniti ruscelli,
starò nella corrente
come un tronco o un cavallo morto,
e finirò incagliato nei pensieri
lungo il delta solitario dello spirito
intricato come il sesso d'una donna.

(1980)

VALERIO MAGRELLI

Tomorrow morning I will take a shower.
Nothing but that is certain.
A future of water and talc
in which nothing follows, and no one
knocks on the door. The crooked
river will fall through the steam, and I
will stand still like a hermit
in the lukewarm rain,
though no visions or temptations
will cross the clouded mirror.
Motionless and silent, traversed
by infinite streams,
I will stay in the current
like a tree trunk or a dead horse,
until I end, stranded in thought,
on the lonely delta of the spirit
as entangled as a woman's sex.

(Dana Gioia)

VALERIO MAGRELLI

Dieci poesie scritte in un mese
non è molto anche se questa
sarebbe l'undicesima.
Neanche i temi poi sono diversi
anzi c'è un solo tema
ed ha per tema il tema, come adesso.
Questo per dire quanto
resta di qua della pagina
e bussa e non può entrare,
e non deve. La scrittura
non è specchio, piuttosto
il vetro zigrinato delle docce,
dove il corpo si sgretola
e solo la sua ombra traspare
incerta ma reale.
E non si riconosce chi si lava
ma soltanto il suo gesto.
Perciò che importa
vedere dietro la filigrana,
se io sono il falsario
e solo la filigrana è il mio lavoro.

(1980)

VALERIO MAGRELLI

Ten poems written in one month
is not much even if this one
will become the eleventh.
Not even the subjects differ greatly
rather there is a single subject
whose subject is the subject, just like now.
This is to say how much
stays off the page,
knocks but cannot enter
nor even has to. Writing
is not a mirror, rather
the rough-surfaced glass of a shower
on which the body falls to pieces
and only its shadow shows through
indistinct but real.
And the one who washes reveals nothing
but his own gestures.
Therefore what purpose is there
in looking beyond the watermark
in case I am a counterfeiter
and the watermark alone is my work?

(Dana Gioia)

Ogni sera chino sul chiaro
orto delle pagine,
colgo i frutti del giorno
e li raduno. Allineati
su filari paralleli corrono i pensieri,
tracce di accorti innesti.
La mia vita è legata
al frugale raccolto,
il suo consumo è quotidiano, dimesso.
Nessuna logica è nel prendere
i fiori o i frutti secchi. L'unica,
e può bastare, è in questa secrezione
spontanea e vegetale dell'idea.
Lenta commozione della terra
che turbata la concepisce. O la cucina
per il suo disadorno commensale.

(1980)

Every evening, bent over the bright
garden of pages,
I gather the fruits of the day
and assemble them. Lined up,
the thoughts run in parallel rows,
the trails of shrewd grafting.
My life is bound
to this frugal harvest,
these humble, everyday commodities.
There is no logic in taking
the dry fruits or flowers. The only reason,
which may suffice, is in this spontaneous
and plant-like secretion of an idea.
The slow stirrings of the troubled earth
which conceives it. Or cooks it
for its plain companions.

(Dana Gioia)

VALERIO MAGRELLI

È specialmente nel pianto
che l'anima manifesta
la sua presenza
e per una segreta compressione
tramuta in acqua il dolore.
La prima gemmazione dello spirito
è dunque nella lacrima,
parola trasparente e lenta.
Secondo questa elementare alchimia
veramente il pensiero si fa sostanza
come una pietra o un braccio.
E non c'è turbamento nel liquido,
ma solo minerale
sconforto della materia.

(1980)

VALERIO MAGRELLI

Especially in weeping
the soul reveals
its presence
and through secret pressure
changes sorrow into water.
The first budding of the spirit
is in the tear,
a slow and transparent word.
Then following this elemental alchemy
thought turns itself into substance
as real as a stone or an arm.
And there is nothing uneasy in the liquid
except the mineral
anguish of matter.

(Dana Gioia)

VALERIO MAGRELLI

Ho finalmente imparato
a leggere la viva
costellazione delle donne
e degli uomini le linee
che uniscono tra loro le figure.
E ora m'accorgo dei cenni
che legano il disordine del cielo.
In questa volta disegnata dal pensiero
distinguo la rotazione della luce
e l'oscillare dei segni.
Così si chiude il giorno
mentre passeggio
nel silenzioso orto degli sguardi.

(1980)

VALERIO MAGRELLI

I have finally learned
how to read the living
constellation of women
and men, to trace the lines
which connect them into figures.
And now I recognize the hints
which bind the disorder of the heavens.
Across this vault designed by thought
I discern light's revolution
and the wavering of signs.
So the day draws to a close
while I walk
in the silent garden of glances.

(Dana Gioia)

VALERIO MAGRELLI

Scivola la penna
verso l'inguine della pagina,
ed in silenzio si raccoglie la scrittura.
Questo foglio ha i confini geometrici
di uno stato africano, in cui dispongo
i filari paralleli delle dune.
Ormai sto disegnando
mentre racconto ciò
che raccontando si profila.
È come se una nube
arrivasse ad avere
forma di nube.

(1980)

VALERIO MAGRELLI

The pen slides
across the groin of the page,
and silently the writing assembles itself.
This sheet has the geometric borders
of an African state on which I set
parallel lines across the dunes.
I am drawing now
while telling this
which in the telling takes its shape.
It is as if a cloud
arrived to take
the form of a cloud.

(Dana Gioia)

VALERIO MAGRELLI

D'estate, come i cinema, io chiudo.
Il pensiero mi vola via e si perde,
il segno si fa vacante,
l'aria è calda
la tavola piena di frutta.

(1980)

Di sera quando è poca la luce,
nascosto dentro il letto
colgo i profili dei ragionamenti
che scorrono sul silenzio delle membra.
È qui che devo tessere
l'arazzo del pensiero
e disponendo i fili di me stesso
disegnare con me la mia figura.
Questo non è un lavoro
ma una lavorazione.
Della carta prima, poi del corpo.
Suscitare la forma del pensiero,
sagomarla secondo una misura.
Penso ad un sarto
che sia la sua stessa stoffa.

(1980)

VALERIO MAGRELLI

In summer, like the theaters, I close up.
Thought flies away from me and gets lost,
the sign goes blank,
the air is warm,
the table stacked with fruit.

(Dana Gioia)

In the evening when the light is dim,
I hide in bed and collect
the silhouettes of reasoning
which silently run across my limbs.
It is here I must weave
the tapestry of thought
and arranging the threads of my self
design my own figure.
This is not work
but a kind of workmanship.
First out of paper, then from the body.
To provoke thought into form,
moulded according to a measure.
I think of a tailor
who is his own fabric.

(Dana Gioia)

VALERIO MAGRELLI

C'è silenzio tra una pagina e l'altra.
La lunga distesa della terra fino al bosco
dove l'ombra raccolta
si sottrae al giorno,
dove le notti spuntano
separate e preziose
come frutta sui rami.
In questo delirio
luminoso e geografico
io non so ancora
se essere il paese che attraverso
o il viaggio che vi compio.

(1980)

VALERIO MAGRELLI

There's silence between one page and another.
The long stretch of the land up to the woods
where gathered
shadows escape the day
and nights show through
discrete and precious
like fruit on branches.
In this luminous
and geographic frenzy
I am still unsure
whether to be the landscape I am crossing
or the journey I am making there.

(Jonathan Galassi)

VALERIO MAGRELLI

Se si scioglie del piombo
e lo s'immerge nell'acqua
se ne hanno figure mostruose.
Il metallo infuocato
si raccoglie in immagini
che verticali scendono sul fondo.
La materia attraversa la fiamma
e il freddo componendo
nel percorso la forma.
Nascono oggetti
irregolari e mobili
fossili e comete, reperti
di geologia domestica.

(1980)

VALERIO MAGRELLI

If you melt some lead
and drop it into water,
you get monstrous figures.
The red-hot metal
gathers itself into shapes
that fall straight to the bottom.
The material crosses the flame
and the cold composes
the form along the route.
Objects are born
irregular and mobile
fossils and comets, evidence
of domestic geology.

(Dana Gioia)

VALERIO MAGRELLI

Cerco una posa della scrittura,
la luce e l'ora in cui ritrarla
e nel disegno descriverne le linee,
il suo diagramma e il grado,
la madre matematica.
Arrivare al verso estremo
senza doverlo dire,
come quei giocatori che gettano
le carte dell'ultima mano
chiudendo la partita senza un termine.

(1980)

VALERIO MAGRELLI

I look for a way of writing,
the light and the hour to draw it forth
and fit the lines into a design,
its diagram and gradation,
its mathematical matrix.
To arrive at the last line
without having to say so,
the way gamblers throw in
the cards from the last hand
and close the round without stopping.

(Dana Gioia)

VALERIO MAGRELLI

Ogni volto fotografato
è un'immagine bellica,
il punto di tangenza
tra l'aereo nemico e la nave
nell'attimo che precede l'esplosione.
Fermo nell'istantanea,
nel contatto flagrante tra due sguardi
immolato, ripreso
mentre le fiamme covano già
nella fusoliera crescendo
dentro i suoi tratti, vive
soltanto il tempo necessario
a compiere la missione del ricordo.

(1987)

VALERIO MAGRELLI

Each photographed face
is an image out of war,
the point of tangency
between the enemy aircraft and the ship
in the moment before the explosion.
Fixed in that instant,
sacrificed in the burning touch
between two glances, then filmed
while the fire smoldering
in the fuselage climbs
inside their features, it lives
only long enough to complete
the mission of remembering.

(Dana Gioia)

VALERIO MAGRELLI

Uno vicino all'altro dopo il pasto
stanno i bicchieri degli sposi, congiunti
in una adiacenza nuziale.
Ovunque, contagiando
vestiti e suppellettili
la coppia tradisce il suo passaggio
e lascia dietro sé
cose abbinate, pari, toccantisi
tra loro, testimoni,
paia del mondo.

(1987)

VALERIO MAGRELLI

Side by side after the meal
the couple's glasses stand, joined
in matrimonial intimacy.
Infecting the clothes and furnishings
in every direction,
the couple betrays its passage
leaving everything behind
linked, matched, touching
one another, witnesses,
a world in pairs.

(Dana Gioia)

VALERIO MAGRELLI

Ho spesso immaginato che gli sguardi
sopravvivano all'atto del vedere
come fossero aste,
tragitti misurati, lance
in una battaglia.
Allora penso che dentro una stanza
appena abbandonata
simili tratti debbano restare
qualche tempo sospesi ed incrociati
nell'equilibrio del loro disegno
intatti e sovrapposti come i legni
dello shangai.

(1987)

VALERIO MAGRELLI

I have often imagined that glances
survive the act of seeing
as if they were poles,
measuring rods, lances
thrown in a battle.
Then I think that in a room
one has just left
those same lines must stay behind
sometimes suspended there and crisscrossed
in the equilibrium of their design
untouched and overlaid like the wooden pieces
in a game of pick-up-sticks.

(Dana Gioia)

VALERIO MAGRELLI

> E la crepa nella tazza apre
> un sentiero alla terra dei morti.
>
> (W.H. Auden)

> ...come quando una crepa
> attraversa una tazza.
>
> (R.M. Rilke)

Ricevo da te questa tazza
rossa per bere ai miei giorni
uno ad uno
nelle mattine pallide, le perle
della lunga collana della sete.
E se cadrà rompendosi, distrutto,
io, dalla compassione,
penserò a ripararla,
per proseguire i baci ininterrotti.
E ogni volta che il manico
o l'orlo si incrineranno
tornerò a incollarli
finché il mio amore non avrà compiuto
l'opera dura e lenta del mosaico.

Scende lungo il declivio
candido della tazza

VALERIO MAGRELLI

> And the crack in the teacup opens
> A lane to the land of the dead.
>   (W.H. Auden)

> ...as when a crack
> crosses a cup.
>   (R.M. Rilke)

I have from you this red
cup with which to drink to all my days
one by one
in the pale mornings, the pearls
of the long necklace of thirst.
And if it drops and breaks, I, too,
will be shattered, but compassionately
I will repair it
to continue the kisses uninterrupted.
And each time the handle
or the rim gets cracked
I will go back to glue it
until my love will have completed
the hard, slow work of a mosaic.

It comes down along the white
slope of the cup

VALERIO MAGRELLI

lungo l'interno concavo
e luccicante, simile alla folgore,
la crepa,
nera, fissa,
segno di un temporale
che continua a tuonare
sopra il paesaggio sonoro,
di smalto.

(1987)

VALERIO MAGRELLI

along the concave interior
and flashes, just like lightning—
the crack,
black, permanent,
the sign of a storm
still thundering
over this resonant landscape
of enamel.

(Dana Gioia)

VALERIO MAGRELLI

Non adottiamo quegli spettacoli
che rinchiudono tristemente poche
persone in un centro oscuro,
tenendole timorose
e immobili nel silenzio e nell'inerzia.

(J.J. Rousseau)

Siedo al cinema, in cura, votato
ad una quieta fisioterapia,
l'esposizione a un chiarore riflesso.
Ferve lo scambio,
cerco la guarigione,
faccio lo schermo dello schermo, cedo
la vasta compresenza del mio corpo
a un'opera lunare. Astante, assente,
sono il paziente della mia passione.
Fermo nel buio condiviso
osservo la discesa della luce,
la sua catabasi.
Sosto in un bosco,
guardo la pellicola di neve
cadere sul paesaggio, sul presepe
di questa notte artificiale, curva
sopra la sala muta
nella corrente del racconto.

VALERIO MAGRELLI

Let's not accept those entertainments
which sadly shut people up in a dark
room, keeping them awe-struck and
immobile in silence and inertia.

(J.J. Rousseau)

I sit, in treatment, at the movies, devoted
to a quiet physiotherapy—
the exposure to reflected brightness.
The exchange heats up,
I seek recovery,
I become the screen on which the screen projects,
I yield the vast presence of my body
to the lunar action. Present, absent,
I am the patient of my passion.
Steady in the co-divided dark,
I watch the light sloping
in its retreat.
Pausing in a wood,
I watch the membrane of snow
fall on the landscape, on the crib
of this artificial night, curved
over the mute hall
in the current of the story.

VALERIO MAGRELLI

Fisso quella finestra illuminata
e scorgo chi passando dietro ai vetri
mi fa segno,
fa segno a questa gente
invalida, malata, messa in posa
per la foto di gruppo.

(1987)

VALERIO MAGRELLI

I gaze at that lighted window
and notice someone passing behind the glass
who signals me,
signals these people
infirm, sick, placed in poses
for a group photograph.

(Dana Gioia)

Se per chiamarti devo fare un numero
tu ti trasformi in numero,
disponi i lineamenti
nella combinazione a cui rispondi.
Il tre che si ripete,
il nove al terzo posto,
indicano qualcosa del tuo volto.
Quando ti cerco
devo disegnare la tua figura,
devo fare nascere le sette cifre
analoghe al tuo nome
finché non si dischiuda la cassa-
forte della viva voce.

Di colpo, mentre sto telefonando,
l'interferenza altera il dialogo,
lo moltiplica, apre una prospettiva
dentro lo spazio buio
dell'udito.
Mi vedo verticale, sonnambolico,
in bilico su una fuga di voci
gemelle, allacciate una all'altra,
sorprese nel contatto.
Sento la lingua della bestia ctònia,

VALERIO MAGRELLI

If I must dial a number to call you,
you transform yourself into a number,
you arrange your features
to answer that combination.
The three which repeats itself,
the nine which comes third,
suggest something of your face.
When I search for you
I must draw your figure
I must bring to birth the seven digits
analogous to your name
until the strong-box of a live
voice unlocks itself.

All at once, while I'm on the telephone,
interference distorts the conversation,
multiplies it, opens a perspective
in the dark space
of hearing.
I see myself upright, sleepwalking,
balanced over a fugue of voices,
twin sisters, tied to each other,
astonished by the contact.
I hear the language of underworld creatures,

VALERIO MAGRELLI

l'orrida treccia di parole, frasi,
   il mostro
policefalo e difforme che chiama me
dalle profondità.

(1987)

VALERIO MAGRELLI

the horrible tresses of words, phrases,
    the many-headed
and deformed monster that calls me
out of the depths.

(Dana Gioia)

VALERIO MAGRELLI

Amo i gesti imprecisi,
uno che inciampa, l'altro
che fa urtare il bicchiere,
quello che non ricorda,
chi è distratto, la sentinella
che non sa arrestare il battito
breve delle palpebre,
mi stanno a cuore
perché vedo in loro il tremore,
il tintinnio familiare
del meccanismo rotto.
L'oggetto intatto tace, non ha voce
ma solo movimento. Qui invece
ha ceduto il congegno,
il gioco delle parti,
un pezzo si separa,
si annuncia.
Dentro qualcosa balla.

(1987)

VALERIO MAGRELLI

I love uncertain gestures:
someone who stumbles, someone else
who bangs his glass,
who can't remember,
gets distracted, or the sentinel
who can't stop the slight flickering
of his lashes—
they matter to me
because in them I see the wobbling,
the familiar rattle
of the ruptured mechanism.
The whole object makes no sound,
has no voice; it only moves.
But here the apparatus,
the play of parts, has given way,
a piece breaks off,
declares itself.
Inside, something dances.

(Jonathan Galassi)

VALERIO MAGRELLI

Questa grafia si logora,
saltano gli angoli, le «erre,»
le «emme,» tornano tonde,
rotolano limate, levigate
pietre nella corrente.
I volti anche,
i volti si consumano
a forza d'esser guardati.
Diventano paesaggi
di rovine.

(1987)

VALERIO MAGRELLI

This handwriting wears itself away,
the corners disappear, the R's,
the M's, become round again;
filed down, they roll away,
polished stones in a stream.
The faces, too,
the faces which waste themselves away
from being watched.
They change into landscapes
of ruin.

(Dana Gioia)

AFTERWORD

New Italian Poets was made possible by the hard work and support of many people in both Italy and America. The notion of an anthology which would present the work of a new generation of Italian poets in English originated with Judith Baumel and Luigi Fontanella during Judy's last year as the Director of the Poetry Society of America. The project found enthusiastic support in Italy, especially from the Centro Internazionale Poesia della Metamorfosi. Meanwhile in the U.S., Elise Paschen, who became the new director of the P.S.A., began the laborious task of early planning.

An editorial committee of both Italians and Americans chose the ten poets included in this volume. The objective was to showcase the work of important poets who had not previously been translated into English at any length. The poets themselves were then contacted and asked to make a representative selection from their work. I was asked by the committee to edit the anthology. I selected the translators, and the long work of translating nearly three thousand lines of poetry began. Once the project was underway and the difficulty of bringing such an immense amount of new work to completion by a set deadline became clear, I asked Michael Palma, whose splendid versions of Guido Gozzano and Diego Valeri I had long admired, to help edit the book. In addition to helping with the editing and translations, Michael has also written nine of the ten critical notes on the poets.

The original vision was to assign one translator for each poet. We hoped thereby to match each Italian voice with an individual American one. This scheme would avoid the confusing anonymity one finds in so many anthologies of translations where too often the voices of individuals blur together in their newly adopted language. Generally, we have preserved this plan. There were a few cases where either the workload was too heavy for one translator or (as with W.S. Di Piero's translations of Fontanella) there were some excellent versions already in existence. Our original scheme also did not count on the dedicated involvement of Stephen Sartarelli, whose energy could not be confined to a single author.

Meanwhile—by happy coincidence—Joseph Parisi, the editor of *Poetry*, informed us that he intended to put together a special double issue devoted to post-war Italian poetry. This ambitious project, co-edited with Paolo Cherchi of the University of Chicago, eventually included the work of 33 poets ranging chronologically from Eugenio Montale (born 1896) to Valerio Magrelli (born 1957). *Poetry*'s special issue covered a broader period of time than our anthology, but there was some overlap. Both Parisi and Cherchi graciously sought the involvement of our translators. Therefore, although virtually every poem in *New Italian Poets* was translated specially for our anthology, about one-fifth of the poems first appeared in *Poetry*'s superb overview of the last half-century of Italian verse.

New Italian Poets represents a major addition to the body of contemporary Italian verse available in English. Almost every poem in this anthology has been translated here for the first time. In several cases, these versions even represent the first attempt to translate any work by the authors into English. None of these translations has ever appeared before in book form. We hope this collection reveals the diversity of poetry being written in Italy today and wins this great living literary tradition a new generation of American readers.

—Dana Gioia

NOTES ON THE TRANSLATORS

BEVERLY ALLEN has been extensively involved in contemporary Italian poetry as a translator, critic, and editor. She is the author of the critical study, *Andrea Zanzotto: The Language of Beauty's Apprentice* (published in Italy as *Andrea Zanzotto: Verso la beltà*). She edited *The Defiant Muse: Italian Feminist Poetry from the Middle Ages to the Present* and *Pier Paolo Pasolini: The Poetics of Heresy*. She has also translated the work of Zanzotto, Spaziani, Amelia Rosselli, and others. Allen is currently a Professor of Italian literature at Syracuse University.

JUDITH BAUMEL is an Assistant Professor of English at Adelphi University where she directs the Creative Writing Program. Her first book of poems, *The Weight of Numbers* (Wesleyan University Press, 1988), won the Walt Whitman Award of the Academy of American Poets. Her reviews of Italian literature have appeared in *The New York Times*. She has also written about American literature for Italian publications.

W.S. DI PIERO is the author of three books of poetry—*The First Hour* (1982), *The Only Dangerous Thing* (1984), and *Early Light* (1985). He has also published a critical collection, *Memory and Enthusiasm: Essays 1975-1985*. Di Piero has done three book-length translations from Italian—the *Pensieri* by Giacomo Leopardi, *This Strange Joy: Selected Poems of Sandro Penna*, and *The Ellipse: Selected Poems of Leonardo Sinisgalli*. He is currently a Professor of English at Stanford University.

RUTH FELDMAN is a poet and translator who lives in Cambridge, Massachusetts, but spends part of every year in Italy. She has published four books of poetry and ten of Italian translations (many in collaboration with Brian Swann), including versions of Lucio Piccolo, Andrea Zanzotto, Rocco Scotellaro, and Primo Levi. She has won the Sotheby's International Poetry Competition Prize, the John Florio Prize for translation, and the Circe-Sabaudia.

JONATHAN GALASSI has published two volumes of translations from the work of Eugenio Montale—*The Second Life of Art: Selected Essays* and *Otherwise: Last and First Poems*. His first collection of poems, *Morning Run*, was published in 1988 by Paris Review Editions. Galassi is the editor-in-chief of Farrar, Straus & Giroux. He is currently working on further translations from Montale's poetry.

DANA GIOIA is a poet and critic whose work frequently appears in *Poetry, The Hudson Review,* and *The New Yorker*. His first collection of poems, *Daily Horoscope,* appeared from Graywolf Press in 1986. His second collection, *The Gods of Winter,* will be published in 1991. He co-edited (with William Jay Smith) *Poems from Italy,* a comprehensive anthology of Italian verse. He has also published a translation of Eugenio Montale's *Mottetti*. Gioia is a businessman in New York.

KENNETH KOCH, the noted poet, is currently a Professor at Columbia University. Among his many volumes of verse are Selected Poems 1950-1982 (Vintage, 1985) and Seasons on Earth (Penguin, 1987). In 1986 he received the Award of Merit in Poetry from the American Academy and Institute of Arts and Letters.

ROBERT McCRACKEN studied at the University of the South at Sewanee, St. John's College (Oxford), and the University of Paris-Sorbonne. He also did graduate work in Comparative Literature at New York University. He received a fellowship to the Jagiellonian University in Cracow, Poland. A poet and translator, McCracken lives in New York City.

MICHAEL PALMA recently won the Italo Calvino award for his translations of Diego Valeri, *My Name on the Wind* (Princeton University, 1989). He also translated *The Man I Pretend To Be: The Colloquies and Selected Poems of Guido Gozzano* (Princeton, 1981). His poems and translations have appeared in *Grand Street, Poetry, Northeast, Paris Review*, as well as several anthologies. His first collection of poems is *The Egg Shape*. He is a Professor of English at Iona College.

STEPHEN SARTARELLI is a well-known translator from French and Italian. Among other works he has translated the Italian novels *The Plague Sower* by Gesualdo Bufalino and *The House on Moon Lake* by Francesca Duranti. He has also published a volume of his own poetry, *Grievances and Other Poems* (Gnossis Press, 1989). Sartarelli is currently translating Stefano D'Arrigo's long novel *Horcynus Orca*.

FELIX STEFANILE is a Professor Emeritus at Purdue University. He has published five books of poetry, most recently *East River Nocturne*. He has also published three book-length translations from Italian poetry—*Umberto Saba: 31 Poems* (1976), *The Blue Moustache: Some Italian Futurist Poets* (1980), and *If I Were Fire: 34 Sonnets of Cecco Angiolieri* (1987). A well-known essayist, Stefanile is also the editor and publisher of Sparrow Press.

LAWRENCE VENUTI is an Assistant Professor of English at Temple University. He edited and translated two volumes of Dino Buzzati's short stories, *Restless Nights* (North Point, 1983) and *The Siren* (North Point, 1984). His versions of Milo De Angelis will be published in the volume *Finite Intuition* by Sun & Moon Press. Venuti has recently received a grant from the NEH to translate I.U. Tarchetti's *Fantastic Tales*.